CATHOLIC APOLOGETICS

A Course in Religion

BOOK IV

"I am the way and the truth and the life." (*John* 14:6).

CATHOLIC APOLOGETICS

GOD, CHRISTIANITY AND THE CHURCH

A Course in Religion

For Catholic High Schools and Academies

BOOK IV

By

Fr. John Laux, M.A.

Late Instructor of Religion, Notre Dame High School, and
Professor of Psychology, Villa Madonna College, Covington, Kentucky.

*"But sanctify the Lord Christ in your
hearts, being ready always to satisfy
everyone that asketh you a reason of
that hope which is in you."*
—1 Peter 3:15

TAN Books
An Imprint of Saint Benedict Press, LLC
Charlotte, North Carolina

Nihil Obstat: Arthur J. Scanlan, S.T.D.
                     Censor Librorum

Imprimatur: ✠ Patrick Cardinal Hayes
                     Archbishop of New York
                     August 27, 1928

Library of Congress Catalog Card No.: 90-70439

ISBN: 978-0-89555-394-2

Cover illustration: A symbolic picture of Our Lord handing over the "keys" of His kingdom to St. Peter, thus establishing him as first Pope.

Printed and bound in the United States of America.

TAN Books
An Imprint of Saint Benedict Press, LLC
Charlotte, North Carolina
2011

About This Series

Fr. John Laux, M.A., was a high school religion teacher who distilled the fruit of his many years of research and teaching into these fine high school religion books. At first glance, it might appear foolish to reprint books that were first published in 1928. But a reading of Fr. Laux's books will lay that thought to rest. For he had a rare talent of capsulizing the intricacies of our Catholic Faith and its theology into succinct, precise, learned and yet lively prose that is at once truly interesting and that all can easily understand. He is profoundly intellectual, yet always clear and easy. His writing, while aimed at the high school student, remains challenging and informative to the college student and the adult Catholic as well. But further, Fr. Laux writes in a virtually undated and almost undateable style, a style that is, one might say, classic and timeless, a style that truly befits his subject matter—the timeless teachings of our Ancient Church. For these reasons, the four books in the high school series are all works of rare genius, as also are his *Introduction to the Bible* and *Church History,* for they all possess these same qualities that make Fr. Laux such a pleasure to read and such a joy to study from.

A Word to the Teacher

The need of some systematic presentation of the truths of our Holy Religion to boys and girls of our American Catholic High Schools has been felt by Catholic educators for a long time. The manuals now in use have been found to be either too technical or too simple, and the problem has been to prepare a text that would suit the needs of the growing mind, and, while enlisting the interest of the pupils in acquiring a knowledge of religious truths, would at the same time encourage the practice of virtue and cultivate a love for the Church.

The present *Course in Religion for Catholic High Schools and Academies* is an attempt to solve this problem. The general arrangement of the course is based, as far as possible, on the division and order of the larger Baltimore Catechism. The catechetical form of presentation has been abandoned, because, in the opinion of prominent educators, "it is conducive to memory work rather than to reasoning, encourages inefficient teaching, and makes almost no appeal to the interest of the pupil."

For practical purposes the work has been divided into Four Parts, each of which is bound and paged separately and provided with copious helps for study and review, a table of contents and an index.

The First Part embraces the mystery of the Trinity, the work of Creation, Redemption, Sanctification, and Consummation. It is introduced by a brief treatment of the nature, necessity, sources, and qualities of the Faith. The Second Part treats of the Means of Grace: the Sacraments, the Sacrifice of the Mass, Indulgences and Sacramentals. Part Three is devoted to General and Special Christian Moral; Part Four to Apologetics.

The writer suggests that every pupil be provided with a copy of the New Testament, to be used throughout the course; a Student's edition of the Missal, to be used in connection with Part Two; and the *Imitation of Christ* a supplementary material for Part Three. It is presupposed that there is a well-stocked Religious Book Shelf in every High School library.

The concluding words of Father Drinkwater's preface to his excellent little book of religious instruction *Twelve and After* are applicable to every textbook in Religion: "Let us remind ourselves that religion is not a book-and-writing matter. Such instruction as this book contains is very useful and in some ways necessary; but there are things even more necessary, such as plenty of singing, corporate prayer, both liturgical and unliturgical and opportunity for personal service, not to speak of the more individual and interior practice of religion. If these more essential things are well managed, then the intellectual instruction will have all the more meaning and fruit. It should become the raw material of Catholic ideals. We can but build up carefully as may be, and then pray for the fire of the Lord to fall in acceptance of the offering."

A word to the teacher of religion. The purpose of the teaching of religion must be the same in all our schools from the grades to the university—to form *religious characters*, to train men and women who will be ready to profess their Faith with firm conviction and to practice it in their daily lives in union with the Church.

This obvious purpose of all religious teaching imposes a twofold duty on the teacher of religion in the High School: to give his pupils a *fuller and more profound grasp of Christian Doctrine*, and to lead them on the *intelligent use* of the helps that have been given us to lead Christian lives.

It is idle to dispute, as is sometimes done, whether the training of the intellect is more important than the training of the heart and the will; the imparting of religious knowledge, than the formation of religious habits. Both are of supreme importance. The will follows the intellect; but the intellect is also powerfully influenced by the will. Ignorance may sometimes be bliss, but never in religious matters. Well-instructed Catholics may become backsliders, but their number is small in comparison with those who are lost to the Church because their ignorance of Catholic teaching made them easy victims of the purveyors of false science, shallow philosophy and neo-pagan morality. Religion requires that the *whole* man worship God with all his faculties and acts. The intellect must *believe* that which is true concerning God—*Faith*; and the *will* must be directed to *do* those actions which are right and to avoid those which are wrong—*Morals*.

Catholic Action is today becoming a vital force throughout the world. The layman cannot effectively engage in Catholic Action unless he is well-versed in the teachings of his faith and able at all times to explain and defend it. The type of layman, therefore, that is needed today is the type which Cardinal Newman asked for years ago when he said: "I want laymen, not arrogant, not rash in speech, not dispositions, but men who know their religion, who enter into it, who know just where they stand, who know what they hold and what they do not; who know their Creed so well that they can give an account of it; who know so much of history that they can defend it. I want an intelligent, well instructed laity. I wish you to enlarge your knowledge, to cultivate your reason, to get an insight into the relation of truth to truth; to learn to view things as they are; to understand how faith and reason stand to each other; what are the bases and principles of Catholicism. Ignorance is the root of bitterness."

The great Cardinal's ideal of the Catholic layman may never be fully attained, but it is certainly worth striving after. It is only through such pious and enlightened laymen and laywomen, working with their bishops and pastors, that Catholic Action can be truly successful. It is the chief duty of our Catholic Educational system to place on the battlefield an army of laymen, equipped to "fight the battles of the Lord."

THE AUTHOR

Acknowledgments

Grateful acknowledgment is made to the following authors and publishers for permission to include copyrighted material from their publications: America Press, for an article in "Thought" by Joseph Rickaby, S.J.; Dolphin Press, "Ketteler and the Christian Reform Movement" by G. Metlake; "Fortnightly Review"; Harcourt, Brace and Company, "Life of Christ" by Giovanni Papini; Longmans, Green and Co., "The Key to the World's Progress" by C. S. Devas, "Three Essays on Religion" by John Stuart Mill; The Macmillan Company, "The Catholic Church and the Appeal to Reason" by Leo Word; John Murphy Company, "Faith of Our Fathers" by Cardinal Gibbons; Charles Scribner's Sons, article in "Scribner's Magazine" by Edwin Grant Conkin; "The Incarnation of the Son of God" by C. Gore; and Joseph F. Wagner, Inc. "The Freedom of Science" by J. Donat, S.J.

Contents

Section III
Reasonableness of Our Belief in the Church

Introduction

The Nature and Value of Apologetics

A. Knowledge and the Sources of Knowledge

1. We possess all our knowledge in the form of judgments. We know something only when we state, at least mentally, that two ideas or concepts, one of which is called the subject, the other the predicate, agree with each other, or do not agree with each other. If I say: "Shakespeare is a dramatist," I assert the agreement of the two concepts "Shakespeare" and "dramatist." If I say: "Men are not angels," I assert the disagreement of the two concepts "men" and "angels."

2. If our judgment is in harmony with reality, it is a true judgment, as "Heat expands iron"; if it is not in harmony with reality, it is a false judgment, as "A circle is not round." If our judgments are uttered without fear of error, they are *certain*; if they are tittered with fear of error, they are *uncertain*, and therefore mere *opinions*. "Twice two is four," is a certain judgment; "Tomorrow will be rainy," is nothing but an opinion.

3. Before making a judgment we must have a reason for doing so. We get our reasons for forming our judgments from what are called the *sources of knowledge*. There are of various kinds:

a) Some truths are in themselves so evident as to be clearly understood by all who have the use of reason, as soon as they are put in words. Such truths are called *self-evident*, because they require no demonstration. For example, when once we understand the meaning of the terms, we cannot fail to grasp that "the whole is greater than its part," or that "the radii of a circle are equal," or that "everything which begins to exist must have been brought into existence by something distinct from itself," or that "what is, is, and cannot at the same time not be."

b) From these self-evident and necessary truths another class of truths is drawn by a *process of reasoning*, that is, not by comparing two concepts directly with each other, but by comparing each with a third, on the principle that two things which are equal to the same thing are equal to each other.

c) Other things we know to he true from the evidence of our *senses*. We can trust our senses unhesitatingly if the sense we are using, e.g., sight or hearing, is in a normal condition and properly applied to the object.

d) Lastly, there are many things which we do not know of ourselves, but which we accept on the *authority* of other people. If our belief rests on the testimony of man, who can err, it is *human faith*; if it rests on the testimony of God, who cannot err, it is *Divine Faith*.

B. Faith and Its Justification

1. To have Divine Faith means to hold firmly and without doubting, all that God has revealed and, through His Church, proposes for our belief. The truths of revelation are the *Object* of Faith; the authority of God, implying infallibility in knowledge, and truth in utterance, is the *Motive* of faith, the reason *why* we believe what God has revealed. The *Church* is the ordinary and infallible means by which we know the truths revealed by God.

Our reason left to itself gives assent only to such judgments as are evidently true. Hence, since the Articles of Faith are not evident, the *will* plays a very important part in the making of an *Act of Faith. Only he can believe who is willing to believe.* The will gives assent to the word of God because it sees in God its highest good. With Simon Peter it says: "Thou hast the words of eternal life" (*John* 6:69). In giving its assent, the will is elevated and strengthened by the *grace of God*. By grace, our Faith becomes *supernatural*; by the assent of the will, it becomes a *free, moral*, and, therefore, *meritorious act*.

2. Our Faith is not an affair of sentiment, a leap in the dark, or an "abdication of our reason"; on the contrary, it is a "seeing faith," a "reasonable service." Every intelligent Catholic should be in a position to justify his Faith at the bar of his reason and his conscience. He must, in other words, be able to form the following judgments:

a) I *may and can* believe these truths proposed for my belief, because God has revealed them;

b) I *must* believe these truths, because God is my supreme Lord and my only salvation.

The first of these judgments, which is called the *judgment of credibility* (*judicium credibilitatis*) rests on three other judgments:

1. *There is a God* who can neither deceive nor be deceived.

"Lord, to whom shall we go? Thou hast
the words of eternal life." (*John* 6:69)

2. *This God has revealed Himself* to us in the Old Testament through the Patriarchs and the Prophets, in the New Testament through Christ and the Apostles.

3. *Christ founded a Church* which He endowed with infallibility for the safeguarding and propagation of Divine Revelation.

These three judgments are called motives of credibility (*motiva credibilitatis*). The first is philosophical, the other two are historical. In the case of the second, viz., that God has revealed Himself to us, it is sufficient to prove that *Jesus Christ is the Son of God and the instrument of Divine Revelation*. He guarantees for us the revelations made in the Old Testament; and by His teaching and the sending of the Holy Ghost on the Apostles, He also guarantees the revelations made through the Apostles.

3. The Mysteries of our Faith cannot be proved from reason and history, because they are beyond reason and therefore incomprehensible.

The divine mysteries," says the Council of the Vatican, "by their own nature so far transcend the created intelligence that, even when delivered by Revelation and received by Faith, they remain covered with a veil of Faith itself, and shrouded in a certain degree of darkness, so long as we are pilgrims in this mortal life, not yet with God.*

In regard to these mysteries we must content ourselves with proving that they are not contrary to reason and that they possess an inestimable value for our souls. It is different with the three truths on which the reasonableness of our Faith rests. The existence of God, the Divinity of Christ, and the divine institution of the Church can be proved by philosophical and historical arguments.

C. Nature and Division of Apologetics

The science which proves the reasonableness of the Catholic Faith is called *Apologetics,* from the Greek word *apologia,* "defense," "justification." "Be ready always," says St. Peter, "to *satisfy* everyone that asketh you a *reason* of that hope which is in you" (*1 Peter* 3:15).

1. Apologetics answers three questions.
1. *Why must we worship God?*
2. *Why must we be Christians?*
3. *Why must we be Catholics?*

2. In our defense of our Faith we have three classes of opponents to deal with.

1. *Atheists, Pantheists, and Materialists*, who deny the existence of a Living, Personal God; i.e. of a Being endowed with intelligence and free will, the First Cause of all things distinct from Himself.

2. *Jews, Mohammedans, Deists (Rationalists), and Indifferentists*, who deny the divine origin of the Christian Religion.

3. *Heretics* of various kinds, who deny one or more articles of the Catholic Faith.

D. The Value of Apologetics

1. Apologetics cannot produce supernatural Faith. Faith is a gift of God. In Baptism God even "gives us the eyes

---

* Vatican Council I (1870) is referred to here. —*Editor,* 1990.

The Harmony of Faith and Reason

with which to see Him." Besides, Apologetics appeals entirely to the intellect, whereas Faith is a matter both of the intellect and the will. "Faith," says St. Thomas, "is an *act of the understanding* adhering to Divine Truth *by command of the will* moved by the grace of God."

2. Apologetics does not claim to be able to prove the foundations of Faith with mathematical certainty. The proposition "The whole is greater than its part" forces conviction on us because the contrary proposition is unthinkable. But the proposition "Jesus of Nazareth arose from the dead" is not evident in the same way. It is an historical statement, the contrary of which is not impossible or unthinkable. The highest kind of certainty we can have in regard to it is that which *excludes all reasonable doubt.* Our proofs are conclusive, but not coercive. They carry conviction to those who consider them with open minds, but not to those who are blinded by passion or prejudice.

"Mathematical propositions," says the French philosopher Malebranche, "are not attacked simply because the human passions are not interested in attacking them. But if the Pythagorean proposition imposed any moral obligation, it would certainly be attacked. If some Academy of Science were to set up the Sixth and Seventh Commandments as scientific propositions, the validity of these propositions would immediately be called in question by all the adulterers and thieves in the world."

3. The real function of Apologetics is twofold. a) to satisfy the intellect of the *honest inquirer*, and, with the aid of grace, to awaken in him the *pius credulitatis affectus*—the pious longing for the Faith; b) to strengthen in the *believer* the resolve never to barter his holy Faith for the shallow theories of a false philosophy or the mess of pottage of a false morality.

> In a letter dated January 6, 1815, Volta, the famous scientist, declares: "I have always believed and still believe the holy Catholic Faith to be the one true and infallible religion. In this Faith I recognize a pure gift of God, a supernatural grace. But I have not neglected those human means which confirm belief and overthrow such doubts as may arise to tempt me. I have given attentive study to the foundations of my Faith. I have read in the works both of defenders and assailants of the Faith arguments for and against it, and have derived thence arguments in its favor which render it most acceptable even to the purely natural reason and prove it to be such that any mind unperverted by sin and passion, any healthy and generous mind, cannot but accept and love it." (Kneller, *Christianity and the Representatives of Modern Science*, St. Louis: B. Herder Book Co., p. 116)

4. In order to profit by the study of Apologetics, we must approach it in the right spirit—the *spirit of humility*; for if there is a God, the attitude of our soul towards Him must necessarily be the humble petition: "Lord, that I may see." And we must purge our hearts from the dominion of the passions, for only the pure of heart shall see God—in this life as well as in the next.

5. The student of Apologetics should heed the admonition of St. Augustine: "We must not want to solve all the difficulties against the Faith before we believe, in order that our life may not come to an end without faith. Simple faith gives us an ever deeper understanding of the things of faith. By faith we subject ourselves to God. If we subject ourselves to God, we shall live right; if we live right, our heart becomes pure; and if our heart is pure, we shall see the truth of what we believe."

SUPPLEMENTARY READING

Faith Is a Gift of God

Faith is a gift of God, and not a mere act of our own, which we are free to exert when we will. It is quite distinct from an exercise of reason, though it follows upon it. I may feel the force of an argument for the divine origin of the Church; I may see that I *ought* to believe; and yet I may be unable to believe. . . . Faith is not a mere conviction in reason, it is a firm assent, it is a clear certainty greater than any other certainty; and this is wrought in the mind by the grace of God, and by it alone. As then men may be convinced, and not act according to their conviction, so may they be convinced, and not believe according to their conviction. . . . In a word, the arguments for religion do not compel anyone to believe, just as arguments for good conduct do not compel anyone to obey. Obedience is the consequence of willing to obey, and faith is the consequence of willing to believe; we may see what is right, whether in matters of faith or obedience, of ourselves, but we cannot will what is right without the grace of God.

—NEWMAN, *Discourses to Mixed Congregations*, p. 224.

The Study of the Science of Apologetics Necessary Especially in Our Day

Though the existence of God is a truth knowable, and easily knowable, by the light of reason, there are many that call that truth in question. Professed Agnostics are perhaps more numerous now than they have ever been before. How to account for this increase in Agnosticism, who can tell? The advances made in physical science can give no clue to it. . . . But whatever the reason may be, Agnosticism is apparently on the increase. It is difficult to avoid contact with Agnostics. They are to be met with in every rank of life. Some of them are aggressive and wish to meet us in discussion. Others profess a wish to believe, and invite us to remove their difficulties. If we ought to be prepared to justify the faith that is in us, much more ought we to be prepared to justify that conviction of God's existence, which is presupposed by all our faith. We ought to be able to defend this conviction against any that might choose to assail it; and

still more ought we to be able to extend a helping hand to such
as might come to us in the spirit of honest inquiry. We say in
a spirit of honest inquiry, for it may very well be that one who
has through no fault of his lost belief in God, is now honestly
endeavoring to find his way back to the truth.
—GILDEA, Introduction to HAMMERSTEIN, *Foundations
of Faith,* St. Louis: B. Herder Book Co., p. ix.

SUGGESTIONS FOR STUDY AND REVIEW

1. In what form do we possess all our knowledge?
2. When are our judgments true? false? certain? uncertain?
3. What is meant by the sources of knowledge?
4. What is meant by self-evident truths? Give examples.
5. How do we acquire knowledge of truths which are not self-evident?
6. When are our senses infallible sources of truth?
7. What is the difference between human and divine faith?
8. Define divine faith. What is its motive? Its object?
9. What part does the will play in the act of faith?
10. Is faith an abdication of reason? Why not?
11. What is meant by the judgment of credibility? On what other judgments does it rest? What are these called?
12. What is our position in regard to mysteries?
13. Define Apologetics. What three questions does it answer?
14. Who are the opponents of the Catholic Apologist?
15. What kind of certainty can we attain in regard to the foundations of our faith?
16. What is the real function of Apologetics?
17. Why should we study Apologetics in the spirit of humility?
18. Write a brief paragraph on each of the following: *Agnostic, St. Thomas Aquinas, Vatican Council, Malebranche, Volta, St. Augustine.* (Consult the *New Catholic Dictionary* or the *Catholic Encyclopedia.*)

CATHOLIC APOLOGETICS

A Course in Religion

BOOK IV

BENE SCRIPSISTI
DE ME THOMA

APOTOEANE

St. Thomas expounds truth with the approbation of the Church

Section I

Reasonableness of Our Belief in God

Chapter I

The Existence of God

A. The Arguments for the Existence of God in General

1. "God, the beginning and end of all things, can be known with certainty from created things by means of the natural light of human reason."

With these words the Vatican Council points to the twofold source of our natural knowledge of God: our natural reason and created things.*

By "created things" we mean the whole realm of nature and the human soul. The contemplation of nature leads us to believe and hope in God, and to love Him; but from the study of our soul, we derive a truer and deeper knowledge of God than from all the rest of creation, because our soul alone is made according to the image and likeness of God.

2. Our natural knowledge of God is indirect, or mediate. We do not see God *immediately*, but only through the medium of His works.

Our knowledge of God, though real, is only *analogical;* that is, our concepts or notions of God are taken from created things and applied to God after we have purified them from all created imperfections and raised them into the sphere of the unlimited and infinite. In other words, we attribute every perfection that exists in the world, such as goodness, justice, knowledge, love, to God, but we say that it exists in Him in a manner more perfect than we can imagine.

---

* Vatican Council I (1870) is referred to here. —*Editor*, 1990.

1

Schilling

God and the Creation

In the beginning God created heaven, and earth. And
the earth was void and empty, and darkness was upon
the face of the deep. And the spirit of God moved over
the waters. . . . And God saw all the things that He had
made, and they were very good. And the evening and
morning were the sixth day. So the heavens and the earth
were finished, and all the furniture of them. And on the
seventh day God ended His work which He had made:
and He rested on the seventh day from all His work which
He had done. And He blessed the seventh day, and sanc-
tified it: because in it He had rested from all His work
which God created and made. (*Gen.* 1:1, 2, 31; 2:1-3).

**3. From the contemplation of nature and the soul we
cannot obtain a full knowledge of God** and His perfections,

because God has communicated the infinite riches of His Being only in a limited manner to the material world and to the human soul. "God *must* be a *mystery*, must be greater than His creation, greater than our intellect and our heart."

> From the material creation we cannot know that there are Three Persons in God. Nor are all the attributes of. God clearly and distinctly revealed in creation. God's holiness and justice, and His Fatherly love for all men, for example, will be fully revealed only in eternity. Our reason tells us that this life is merely a preparation for a future life in which the good will be rewarded and the wicked punished; but supernatural revelation alone gave us complete certainty on this all-important matter. Through the life, teaching, and death of Christ we know that God is love, in spite of all the suffering and misery in the world; and that God is holy and just, in spite of the apparent happiness of the sinner in this life.

4. The various arguments by which our reason proves conclusively the existence of God may be divided into two groups: 1) those which are derived from the contemplation of the visible world; 2) those which are derived from the consideration of the human soul. Each group embraces two arguments.

First Group. a) The first thing that strikes us when contemplating the universe is its *wonderful orderliness* and *purposeful arrangement*. The universe is a most marvelous work of art, which must have been planned and executed by an all-wise and all-mighty Master. This is called the *Teleological Argument*, from the Greek word *telos*, end or purpose.

b) From the very existence of the world, from the movement and life in the world, we infer the existence of some Cause different from it and superior to it, of some original giver of life and motion. This is called the *Cosmological Argument*, from the Greek word *kosmos*, world.

Second Group. Man is by nature both a *religious* and a *moral* being. From the examination of the religious nature of man, we derive what is known as the *Historical Argument;* and from the consideration of his moral nature, the *Moral Argument* for the existence of God.

All these arguments for God's existence are based on the *Law of Causality*: "Anything which begins to exist must have been brought into existence by something distinct from itself." This law or principle needs no proof. It shines by its own light.

B. The Teleological Argument
or The Reign of Law in the Universe

1. We are all familiar with the ideas conveyed by the words *order* and *plan*. They are so closely related to each other that we can call them correlative ideas. Wherever there is order, there is plan. For wherever there is an arrangement of means to attain an end, we say that order exists; and the arrangement of means to attain an end is precisely what is meant by the word *plan*.

Our reason tells us that wherever there is order and plan, an intelligent being has been or is at work. This is true of the simplest household utensil as well as of the most complicated industrial machinery. And the more complicated the plan, the greater is the intelligence that it supposes, because every effect must have a proportionate cause. The plan exists first in the mind of the artist or the engineer, who then communicates it to, or, we might say, impresses it upon, the raw material.

This necessary connection between order and plan, between design and designer, is the *basis* of the teleological argument for the existence of God.

We have only to look around us to see that the universe is full of natural works of art which in beauty, variety, grandeur, and perfection far surpass the highest achievements of human craftsmanship.

From these facts we can draw only one conclusion: the universe is the work of a Supreme Intelligence, a Master-Artist, whom we call God.

2. The facts on which our argument rests are countless. Every new discovery in the field of the natural sciences— in astronomy, in physics and mechanics, in chemistry and biology, in botany and zoology—furnishes us with new wonders of Divine Workmanship. The *laws of nature are nothing but the order existing among things and perceived by the mind of man.* Organic nature, above all, reveals itself to us as a vast kingdom in which order and design reign supreme.

3. Space prevents us from entering into details; any work on general science will supply them. But we must say a word in regard to the *beauty of the universe,* which simply cannot be explained except as the work of an ordering intelligence.

"Beauty is present everywhere in nature. Whether we look at the sky above us, or at the earth below, or at the wide expanse of waters, all manifest it. They display it in all their parts and under all their aspects. It is seen in the smallest flower, no less than in the forest as a whole: in the icebound regions of the pole, and in the sandy deserts, as in the glories of the tropics. Nor is it color alone that is in question. The forms of nature possess the same quality. The outlines of the different kinds of trees, the configuration of their leaves, the varied curves of their branches are as perfect in their way as is the coloring of the flowers. Of the innumerable species of animals which people earth and air and sea there is hardly one which does not arouse our wondering admiration, some by their grace, some, like the lion and the elephant, by their grandeur. Moreover, the sense of hearing, no less than that of sight, acknowledges the perfection of nature's handiwork. The song of the birds, the music of the waters, the sound of the breeze among the trees attract and delight us. We recognize beauty as the authentic note of nature in all its works." (Joyce, *Principles of Natural Theology*, p. 127.)

4. The Teleological Argument has been challenged by unbelievers since the days of the Greek philosopher Epicurus and the Latin poet Lucretius. *Epicurus* (d. 270 B.C.) attributed the order and purpose everywhere observable in the universe to the accidental coming together of atoms; in other words, he made *Blind Chance* the Designer of the universe. *Cicero* answered him: "If anyone supposes that this most beautiful and glorious world was made by the accidental coming together of atoms, I do not understand why he should not suppose that the *Annals* of Ennius might be produced by pouring out on the earth the twenty-one letters of the alphabet in countless profusion."

> The French philosopher *Diderot* thought that this was possible. He maintained that if a case of type were emptied out a sufficient number of times, the letters might at last so fall as to give the text of the *Iliad*. Of course such an idea is absurd. Order cannot result from disorder. Where there is order, whether in the *Iliad* of Homer or in the movements of the heavenly bodies, that order must have a sufficient reason; and blind chance is not such a sufficient reason. The atoms of Epicurus could whirl around in space for billions of years without ever producing an oak tree, much less a human eye or ear or heart.

5. Blind Chance, discredited for centuries by all thinking men as a possible Organizer of the universe, was raised on the throne once more by *Charles Darwin* and his school. Darwin contended that what we regard as standing proofs of the creative skill of a Supreme Intelligence could be accounted for by the *sole operation of physical causes.* "Inconceivably long periods of time," "Natural Selection," "Survival of the Fittest," "Struggle for Life" were the magic phrases invented to support his theory. According to this theory, nature's causes operate blindly: "there is not in them any inherent determination guiding them in one direction rather than another." Thus, we see that Darwinism harks back to the Blind Chance of Epicurus; and we may add that it is as dead today as the old Greek philosopher's theory of the "accidental coming together of atoms." Natural Selection does not explain the origin of species nor the origin of anything else.

> "Only a madman," writes Dr. A. V. Hill, a Nobel prize man in medicine, "would attribute a telephone system purely to laws of chance and the principles of Natural Selection, and only ignorance or fanaticism could attribute a living cell to the same laws of chance and the principles of Natural Selection." (*Living Machinery*).
>
> How can the struggle for life and the survival of the fittest in this struggle explain the curious fact that many animals have the powers to replace or *regenerate* new parts if the old ones are lost? "If the common *flatworm* be cut transversely, the head end will regenerate a new tail, and the tail will regenerate a new head. If the *crab* loses a leg, a new one is regenerated. The same is true of the *cockroach* before the final molt. If one or more arms are torn from the *starfish*, they are replaced with new ones" (Wieman, *General Zoology*, p. 29). According to the Darwinian theory, these mutilated animals would have to perish in the struggle for life.

6. But, it will be objected, are there not many things in nature which have no purpose whatever, such as rudimentary organs, suppressed and degenerated, aimless and inactive parts of the body? And are not these fatal to the idea of purpose in nature, to the idea of an Intelligent Supreme Being?

We answer with Professor Huxley: "If we are to assume, as evolutionists generally do, that useless organs dwindle away by disuse, such cases as the existence of rudiments of toes in the foot of a horse place us in a dilemma. For, either these rudiments are of no use to the animal, in which case, considering that the horse has existed in its present form since the Pliocene epoch, they surely ought to have disappeared; or they are of some use to the animal, in which case they are of no use as arguments against Teleology." Sixty years ago the thyroid gland in the throat was supposed to be absolutely without use. Now we know that it plays a very important part in the human body, and that its failure to function brings about a condition closely allied to idiocy. In time science will, no doubt, discover uses for all the other so-called "aimless and inactive parts" of the animal body.

7. Again, it is objected: **The prodigality of nature, the constant enormous waste in the vegetable world, the presence of vermin and harmful insects, of disease-carrying flies, mosquitoes, and bacteria, the sufferings of animals and men, seem to argue against the wisdom of the Designer of the universe.** This is a favorite argument of the materialists of all times.

We answer: No believer in God maintains that he knows *all* the purposes of the Creator. As our knowledge of nature's laws increases we see purpose and design at work where our forefathers looked for them in vain. The so-called defects in the work of the Designer are not due to the imperfect character of His design, but to our imperfect understanding of it.

a) The presence of *vermin* of every kind must not be judged by the amount of molestation it causes us. That is evidently not its purpose. The sucking organ of the bedbug is a contrivance of marvelous design, just as the human body. The *seeds,* the life-germs, so prodigally scattered about by nature are not all destined for reproduction, but also to a very large extent for the nourishment of men and animals. The lavish "waste" of fern spores buried in the ground ages ago has given us coal, to which so much of our material civilization is due.

b) The existence of *pain and suffering* in the world is the greatest problem that faces us when we reflect on God and His relation to the world. Let us deal first with the sufferings of animals.

We cannot form any accurate notion of what these sufferings are. We have no means of estimating to what extent animals feel. One thing seems to be certain: the degree of their suffering is very different from our own. "Brutes feel far less than man, because they cannot reflect on what they feel; they have no advertence or direct consciousness of their sufferings. And, hence, as their other feelings, so their feeling of pain is but faint and dull in spite of their outward manifestations of it. It is the intellectual comprehension of pain as a whole, diffused through successive moments, which gives it its special power and keenness, and it is the intellectual soul only, which the brute has not, which is capable of that comprehension" (Newman). Since animals do suffer to some extent, it is detestable to add unnecessarily to their sufferings; but the sentimentalism that treats animal pain as an evil as great as human suffering is unreasonable and ridiculous. Animals do prey on one another, a cat does play with the mouse before devouring it, and the big fishes live on the little fishes; animal life is, in fact, as the poet says, a record of rapine and slaughter. But is there anything in the nature of the brute animal, as far as we can see, that points to the conclusion that it has any other destiny than to serve as food for other animals or for man?

Death has not the same sting for the animal as for man. The animal lacks that which makes death so dreadful for man—the foreknowledge of it. Someone has well said that a sudden and violent death is better for the animal than a slow death through old age, because there is nothing in the animal nature to make old age either beautiful or desirable.

We sometimes speak of the *cruelty of animals*. But this is not true. Man is cruel, not the animal. Man often tortures his fellowman and gloats over his sufferings. Not so the beast or bird of prey; nature has given it weapons and instruments to bring death to its victim quickly and surely.

But why is there pain and suffering at all in the world? Could not an Almighty Creator have made His creatures immune to pain? We answer by asking another question: Could corporeal beings with bodily organs capable of sensation feel pleasure if they could not feel pain? They could not, unless God worked a perpetual miracle to keep pain away from them—they would have to be sentient at one moment in order to be able to feel pleasure, and not sentient the next moment in order not to feel pain. Since it is clear that the pleasure of animal existence far exceeds the pain, it is not incompatible with God's wisdom and goodness to permit the one for the sake of the other.

When we come to man, the problem of physical evil assumes larger proportions. Man suffers incalculably more than the lower animals, and physical evil is aggravated and intensified by moral evil, or *sin*. We must not, however, forget that, in the case of men, suffering is raised into the domain of the *spiritual and the moral;* in him it loses the transitoriness that characterizes it in the animal kingdom. Pain and suffering are factors that contribute largely to the moral edifice of humanity. Untold blessings spring from sacrifice, and moral good is worth all the sacrifices that can be made for it. Pain becomes a *stimulus* and a helper. God makes use of physical evil to punish and to refine individuals and nations, as gold is refined by fire. *"Sanabiles fecit nationes"*—"He made the nations of the earth healable" (*Wis.* 1:14). What appears to us shortsighted mortals a hindrance and a check is in reality a lever in the hand of God to raise us to unimagined heights of moral goodness. The most glorious revelations of God's justice and love as well as the most heroic virtues of His creatures presuppose the existence of physical and moral evil, of sin and suffering. The heroism of duty, the overpowering splendor of unselfish deeds, loyalty to God even unto the sacrifice of life itself, in a word, all that is great and noble and lovable in saints and heroes, presupposes the conflict between good and evil. It needed a Nero, and such as he, to call forth the heroic virtue displayed by the martyrs. The worst deed of the Jewish people, the murder of the Messias, resulted in the greatest blessing for mankind.

> Si tollis hostem, tollis et pugnam;
> Si tollis pugnam, tollis et coronam;
> Si tollis libertatem, tollis et dignitatem.
> St. Columban

"Without an adversary there is no conflict, and without a conflict there is no crown; without freedom no honor."

"We cannot raise the question: How can there be evil if God exists? without raising the second, How can there be good if He exist not?" (Boethius).

Natural reason can never adequately "justify the ways of God to man"; the existence of physical, and moral evil in the world will always remain the greatest of the world's mysteries. Christianity alone offers a satisfying explanation. "It tells us of the fall of man and its consequences, and of the Redemption through Christ. It tells us of the glorious promise that all nature shall one day be transfigured. It guides struggling and suffering humanity to Him who cast the wood of the cross into the bitter waters of tribulation in order to sweeten them; to Him whose instrument of torture and death is raised

up before the world as the sign of salvation from sin, and sorrow, and death"; to Him who showed that "the problems of sin
and suffering are really one, for sin can be healed by suffering, and sorrow itself can be turned into joy."

C. The Cosmological Argument
or God and the Origin of the Universe

**1. In our experience every event (effect) is determined
by a cause.** That cause is in its turn determined by another
cause. But we cannot assume an infinite series of causes, because
an infinite series with no beginning involves a contradiction. And
even if we did suppose the possibility of an infinite series, that
would not explain how causation began. Hence there must be an
uncaused Cause, the ultimate Cause of all the events which proceed from it. *This ultimate and supreme Cause we call God.*

> The series of causes in the universe is like a chain to
> which new links are continually added. There is always
> a last link to which the succeeding one is attached. But
> if it has a last link, an end, it must also have a begin-
> ning, a first link, which carries all the other links but is
> itself carried by none. "In this chain we must of neces-
> sity go back to that first link which is fastened to the
> throne of God" (Secchi).

**2. The mind refuses to entertain the idea that noth-
ing should turn into something.** It is evident that if there
ever had been nothing, there could never have been anything.
As a matter of fact, all philosophers and scientists agree that
there must be an *eternal, absolute, self-sufficient, necessary Being.*
They part company, however, when the practical question is
asked: What is this absolute, self-sufficient Being?

The *Pantheist* answers: "We ourselves and all around us are
merely the manifestation of one and the same Substance, one
original Force that thinks in man, seizes its prey in a wild
beast, unfolds bud and leaf in an oak, darts through the clouds
in lightning, strikes the cliff in a storm wave."

The *Materialist* answers: "We ourselves and all around us,
earth and all the stars, are due to chance, the product of whirling
Atoms, how arisen, how ending, known to none."

The *Theist* answers: "All has arisen from the *fiat* of an intelligent Creator, and all exists in consequence with a definite
purpose" (C. S. Devas, *The Key to the World's Progress,* New

York: Longmans, Green and Co., Section 9).

Pantheism and Materialism agree in reducing All to One. For this reason both systems have been given the common name *Monism*—from the Greek *monos,* "single." To distinguish them, Pantheism has been called *Spiritualistic Monism,* while the term *Materialistic Monism* has been applied to Materialism. According to Pantheism, "all reality is one spiritual being, or rather a being that is neither spirit nor matter but such that matter and spirit are alike but aspects of him or it." According to Materialism, there exists but one *Thing,* that which we usually call Matter, of which mind or spirit is only a form. Both agree in rejecting the reality of a personal God, and therefore both are irreconcilably opposed to *Theism,* which emphatically affirms the existence of a personal God distinct from the universe which He created and governs.

3. Pantheism does not explain the origin of the universe; for if, as Pantheism affirms, God is not really distinct from the world, the world is without a cause. Besides, Pantheists are involved in a glaring contradiction: They must admit that the same universe is necessary, eternal, absolute, and self-sufficient in so far as it is identified with God, but contingent, finite, not self-existent and self-sufficient in so far as it is the universe.

Pantheists contradict the testimony of consciousness. If there is one thing that we are more conscious of than another, it is that we do not naturally share in the Divine Nature, that we are not God. "Strange truth," a French philosopher-poet says of Pantheism, "hard to conceive, humiliating alike for the heart and the brain, that the universe, that we all should be God, and not know it."

4. If Pantheism cannot explain the origin of the universe, much less can Materialism. The Materialists of our day are the worthy successors of the "Night-Philosophers," of whom Aristotle speaks, "who made night the cause of day, and nothing the mother of being." They set up *Matter,* the world of whirling atoms, as the eternal necessary being, the cause of all that is. It was surely the strangest aberration of the human mind, to use the words of a modern philosopher, when Materialism placed the Atom on the throne of God.

Matter cannot be self-existent from all eternity. For, something which exists necessarily and of its own right, which possesses in itself the reason of its existence, must also be absolutely perfect and independent of conditions outside itself. Matter is anything but that. If nothing but dead matter existed

Aristotle

in the beginning, as Materialists claim, we should have nothing but dead matter now. For, according to all observation and experiment, matter cannot set itself in motion, cannot produce organic life, sensitive life, consciousness, reason, thought, speech, moral goodness, order, beauty.

5. Riddles of the Universe. One of the most eminent scientists of the last century, Professor du Bois-Reymond, found that there are seven Enigmas or *Riddles of the Universe;* that is, seven things which are matters of daily experience, but which can never be explained if we recognize no other god than Matter. These Riddles are:

1. What is Matter and Force?
2. What is the cause of Motion?
3. What is the origin of Life?
4. What produces Sensation and Consciousness?
5. What produces rational Thought and Speech?
6. What is the cause of Order and Design in Nature?
7. What is Free Will?

6. Let us examine two of these enigmas more closely: the origin of Motion and of Life. We shall see that neither can be accounted for unless we admit the existence of a Prime Mover who is Himself unmoved, and of a Creator of Life.

a) By *Motion,* we understand *all changes that take place in* things. Materialists claim that Motion is an original property of matter, that matter always has been and always will he in uninterrupted movement and transformation. But this is in direct opposition to the first of *Newton's Laws,* which are universally recognized as the most firmly established and unquestionable of all scientific conclusions. This law tells us that a body at rest will continue at rest forever unless compelled by some force to move, just as a body in motion will continue to move at the same rate and in the same direction unless compelled by force to arrest or alter its course. Upon the universal certainty of this law the whole of our Natural Philosophy depends: but it absolutely blocks the way for the idea that Matter has an innate tendency to move itself, which is thus quite unscientific. Not self-movement but *Inertia* is the property which science ascribes to Matter (Gerard, *The Old Riddle and the Newest Answer*, p. 14).

From this it follows that all movement or change must proceed from some Motive Power that is not itself set in motion, that is not subject to change. This Power we call God.

b) It is a fact, vouched for by all men of science without exception, that there was a time when there was no life on earth. *Geology* points to epochs in the formation of the earth when life was impossible and when no vestige of it is to be found.

Since life did not and could not always exist on the earth, it must originally have either sprung from lifeless matter or been put there by someone.

The first alternative has long since been abandoned by science. *Omne vivum e vivo, omnis cellula e cellula, omnis nucleus e nucleo*—Every living thing comes from a living parent, every life-cell from another life-cell, from organic matter alone can the smallest particle of organic matter be derived. This is one of the most conclusive results of modern research. (Louis Pasteur). So-called *spontaneous generation*—that is, the production of life from lifeless matter—is a figment of the imagination.

Hence there remains only the other alternative, viz., that life is the result of a special act of creation, that there is a Giver of life, who is Life Itself—the *Living God.*

"To invite me to agree to mechanism (materialism) as an explanation of life phenomena, is to ask me to bury my head in the sand and pretend that things are not there when I know they are." (A. V. Hill, *Living Machinery.*)

Lord Kelvin suggested that a life-germ may have fallen from some other star upon our earth. But even if that were the case, it is no solution of the problem of life; it only puts the question a stage farther back.

7. We sometimes hear it said: Creation is impossible, because *ex nihilo nihil fit*—**nothing is made out of nothing.**

We answer: To imagine creation to be the ghostlike appearance on the scene of *something* where there was previously *absolutely nothing,* is, of course, absurd. But no sane person imagines such a thing. Creation supposes an almighty God at the beginning of the world, who called all things into being by an act of His will without making use of any pre-existing matter.

D. The Moral Argument
or God in Conscience

1. The Facts. We know from experience that we have naturally a *conscience.* We have, in the first place, a *sense of right and wrong.* We call some thoughts, words, and deeds good, others bad. We have, moreover, a *sense of a moral obligation imposed upon us.* We must avoid evil and do good. This obligation is so strong that we feel remorse and compunction when we have done wrong, whilst our good actions are invariably followed by self-approval, inward peace, and lightness of heart.

It is also a fact that conscience is something *common to all men.* No normal human being is without a knowledge of the first principles of morality. In all men, too, conscience speaks with an authority that cannot be gainsaid. It is an absolute monarch, an impartial supreme judge. It rewards and punishes on the spot.

It is true that in some men we cannot find a trace of conscience. But such men are afflicted with *moral insanity:* they are exceptions which prove the rule.

2. Explanation of the Facts. Whilst the rest of creation is subject to the laws of nature, man is *free.* But his liberty is not without a check. The commands "Thou shalt" and "Thou shalt not" are clearly and distinctly traced on his consciousness. He knows that he is free to disregard them; but he also knows that, if he does, he must pay the penalty.

This *natural law of man's moral nature* points as inevitably to God as do the laws which govern the universe. God has impressed His mind and His will, not only on the organic and inorganic world, on matter and its forces, but also on the soul of man and its powers.

Hence, men have always recognized the voice of conscience, not as their own, but as God's voice; its sovereignty and power as the sovereignty and power of God.

3. It has been justly remarked of the *argument from conscience* that it has the advantage of leading us more directly than any other to a true conception of a just, holy, and merciful God. It has been admirably drawn out by Cardinal Newman in his *Grammar of Assent,* pp. 98-117. We can quote only a few characteristic sentences:

"If, as is the case, we feel responsibility, are ashamed, are frightened, at transgressing the voice of conscience, this implies that there is One to whom we are responsible, before whom we are ashamed, whose claims upon us we fear. If, on doing wrong, we feel the same tearful, broken-hearted sorrow which overwhelms us on hurting a mother; if, on doing right, we enjoy the same sunny serenity of mind, the same soothing, satisfactory delight which follows on our receiving praise from a father, we certainly have within us the image of some person to whom our love and veneration look, in whose smile we find our happiness, for whom we yearn, towards whom we direct our pleadings, in whose anger we are troubled and waste away.

"These feelings in us are such as require for their exciting cause an intelligent being: we are not affectionate towards a stone, nor do we feel shame before a horse or a dog; we have no remorse or compunction on breaking mere human law: yet, so it is, conscience excites all these painful emotions, confusion, foreboding, self-condemnation; and, on the other hand, it sheds upon us a deep peace, a sense of security, a resignation, and a hope, which there is no sensible, no earthly object to elicit.

"'The wicked flees, when no one pursueth.' Then, why does he flee? Whence his terror? Who is it that he sees in solitude, in darkness, in the hidden chamber of his heart?

"If the cause of these emotions does not belong to this visible world, the Object towards which his perception is directed must be Supernatural and Divine; and thus the phenomena of Conscience, as a dictate, avail to impress the imagination with the picture of a Supreme Governor,

Cardinal Newman

a Judge, holy, just, powerful, all-seeing, retributive, and
is the creative principle of religion, as the Moral Sense
is the principle of Ethics." (pp. 106-107).

**4. But may not what we call conscience be the result
of education and environment, as we hear and read so
often today?**

If conscience is wholly the result of environment, how comes
it that the first principles of morality are held equally by the
Hottentots, the American Indians, the Esquimaux and the cul-
tured white men of Europe and America, although their environment is so totally different? If conscience is wholly the result
of education, why does it so often rebel against the very things
which it is taught? Conscience is not the result of education,
but a factor which the educator finds ready-made and which
he tries to develop like the other faculties and powers of his
pupils. Conscience is often led astray by ignorance and want

of proper training, by false principles and bad example; yet it makes itself felt in spite of all these hindrances and can never be completely stifled.

E. The Historical Argument or Man's Need of God

1. The Facts. All races, civilized and uncivilized, are at one, and have ever been at one, in holding that the facts of nature and the voice of conscience compel us to affirm the existence of God. *Religion*—that, is, the knowledge of God, of His will, and of our duties towards Him—not *Materialism,* is an inalienable possession of the human race. Religion belongs to man's nature just as truly as thought and free will, language, customs, and art.

There is no race of men without religion. It used to be confidently asserted, especially by the Materialistic evolutionists of the last century, that savage tribes existed destitute of all religious notions, and that man in his original state had no religion whatever. Today all anthropologists agree that "there are no races however rude which are destitute of all idea of Religion." (Jevons, *Introduction to the History of Religion,* p. 7.)

Since the days of Darwin, the Patagonians of Tierra del Fuego were regarded as a horde of cannibals without any articulate language and without any notions of religion. In 1921 two missionaries of the Society of the Divine Word, Fathers Gussinde and Koppers, were admitted to the initiation ceremonies by which the full privileges of manhood are conferred on the youths. They were astonished at what they heard and saw. Such names as "My Father," the "Highest," the "Strong One," the "Almighty," the "Ancient One in Heaven," were applied to the God worshiped by the people. Before retiring to rest, a father said to his son: "May the heavenly Father grant us all to see a new and happy day." Before setting out on a journey, a young man was heard to say: "If my Father is good to me and protects me, I shall return." Far from being cannibals, these people would not even eat the flesh of animals such as foxes, dogs, and rats, which occasionally eat human flesh.

2. Explanation of the Facts. The fact that the overwhelming majority of mankind have at all times firmly believed in the existence of God clearly proves that *man is by nature religious.*

Man needs God, aspires after Him, seeks union with Him. Man is religious in his intellect, for even the rudest savages recognize God as the creator and ruler of all things. He is *religious also in his will,* for he sees in God the author and avenger of the moral law. Thus, the voice of man's nature proclaims the existence of God, and this utterance must be true. "What all men, impelled as it were by instinct, hold to be true, is a natural truth," says Aristotle.

Man as an individual needs God; he also needs Him as a social being. Society without God is a house "builded on the sand." Many years ago, a Spanish statesman described the consequences of materialistic teaching in the following words: "The professor, who has patented his own wisdom, proclaims from his chair in the university: 'There is no God.' The ruler in his palace hears the news with astonishment and hastens to apply it to his own conscience and says: 'There is no justice.' It finds an echo in the ears of the criminal and he says to himself: 'There is no guilt.' Flaming youth hears it and draws the logical conclusion: 'There is no virtue.' It comes to the knowledge of the subject, and he argues correctly: 'There is no law.' When it reaches the streets of the city, blood flows, and above the roar of the cannon and the rattle of musketry we hear the howl of the mob: 'Away with God, Heaven, and Eternity.'"

Without God marriage is without dignity, the family without authority, education without its highest appeal, the State without a basis for law and right. Just as science and philosophy have never been able to disprove the existence of God, so they have never found a substitute for Him. The French Revolution, which in 1793 abolished the worship of God and placed the goddess of Reason on the desecrated altars, was compelled in the following year to introduce the "Feast of the Supreme Being."

F. The Nature and Attributes of God

Every argument for the existence of God gives us some insight into the *Nature of God.*

1. God is a Self-existent Being. Such a Being cannot be matter like our bodies, nor force like electricity. It must be *Spirit.* Not Something, but Someone. Not impersonal, but a Personal Being. **God is a Pure Spirit.**

2. A Self-existent Being must necessarily stand *alone,* above and beyond all other beings, who derive their being from Him. **There is but one God.**

3. A Self-existent Being exists of necessity, and therefore *always existed.* There can be no past nor future with God, because He is outside of time. For Him there can be only an ever-present Now. **God is Eternal.**

4. A Self-existent Being cannot be subject to change, for all change implies imperfection in the subject capable of change. But there can be no imperfection in God. **God is immutable.**

5. A Self-existent Being, from whom all other being is derived, must be present wherever anything is or can be; and He must be present everywhere, not only by His Power, but also by His Substance; for power, as Newton remarks, cannot subsist without substance. **God is omnipresent.**

> We must not represent to ourselves the Divine Omnipresence as a sort of *infinite extension.* We might rather conceive it, St. Augustine suggests, as we conceive the truth "Twice two equals four" everywhere. This truth is independent of all limitations of time and space. It is whole and undivided everywhere. It would be present without change to the minds of myriads of other worlds if they should be created at this moment. It would receive them into its presence rather than they it, and would no more be bounded by their limits than it was before. Now in place of this abstract truth, say the same of the Substantial Truth, God, and you will have a true concept of His immensity or omnipresence.

6. A Self-existent Being, from whom all law and order in nature, and intellect and free will in man are derived, must be supereminently **endowed with Understanding and Free Will,** otherwise He would be inferior to His own creatures.

7. A Self-existent Being must be infinite in all perfection. Infinite means without limits. Perfections are all good qualities we know of or can imagine. God, being the cause of all that is good and desirable in creation, all the good in things must be in Him first, and without limit. If it is not in Him first, He could not be the cause of it in His creatures; if it is not in Him without limit, He is on the same plane as His creatures—which is absurd. He must, therefore, be infinitely powerful, wise, good, beautiful, holy, just, merciful, patient, true, faithful.

8. Since we are finite, limited, and God is infinite, unlimited, it follows that God must ever remain **infinitely incomprehensible** to us. "It is impossible," says St. Augustine, "thoroughly to grasp and comprehend God; for couldst thou

comprehend Him, He would not be God." The wonder is, not
that we know so little about God, but that we know so much
about Him. "Instead of complaining that God has hidden Himself, you will give Him thanks for having revealed so much of
Himself." (Pascal.)

The Teleological Argument Briefly Stated

"We see that many things possessing no knowledge, namely
physical objects, act towards a goal; which follows from the fact
that they are always or almost always active in the same way
in order to attain that which is best. From this it follows that
they attain their goal not by accident but *purposively*. But that
which has no knowledge tends towards a goal only through
guidance by a being that has knowledge and reason, like the
arrow of the archer. Hence an intelligent being exists by whom
all things of nature are directed towards their goal, and this
we call *God*."

—St. THOMAS AQUINAS, *Summa Theologica*, I, q. 2, a. 3.

The Cosmological Argument as Formulated by St. Thomas

We see some things in the world that could either be or not
be, since things come into being and disappear, whence it is
possible for them to be and likewise not to be. But it is impossible that everything of such a nature exist forever, since that
which can also not be, at some time is not.

Now if all things whatsoever are capable of not being, then
there was at one time nothing actual. But if that were true, neither would there be anything at present. For that which is not,
begins to be only by means of something that is. In the case,
then, of there being nothing actual, it would be impossible for
anything to come into existence; and there would now be nothing, which is evidently false. Hence not everything that is, is
merely possible; there must be a *necessary being* among things.
But every necessary being has the ground of its necessity either
from elsewhere or not. For this, it is again impossible to proceed

St. Thomas' victory over error

ad infinitum in regard to the necessary beings that have the ground of their necessity elsewhere, just as this is impossible in regard to efficient causes. Consequently we must accept something that is *necessary in itself,* and has not received the ground of its necessity elsewhere, being rather the cause of necessity in others. And this all call *God. —Summa Theologica*, I, q. 2, a. 3.

Science and the Teleological Argument

Science has destroyed many old traditions but it has not destroyed the foundations of ethics or religion. In some respects it has greatly contributed to these foundations.

The universality of natural law has not destroyed faith in God, though it has modified many primitive conceptions of deity. This is a universe of ends as well as of means, of teleology as well as of mechanism. Mechanism is universal but so also is finalism. It is incredible that the system and order of nature, the evolution of matter and worlds and, life, of man and consciousness and spiritual ideals are all the results of chance. The greatest exponents of evolution, such as Darwin, Huxley, Asa Gray, and Weisman, have maintained that there is evidence of some governance and plan in nature. This is the fundamental article of all religious faith. If there is no purpose in the universe, or in evolution, or in man, then indeed there is no God and no good. But if there is purpose in nature and in human life, it is only the imperfection of our mental vision that leads us sometimes to cry in despair: "*Vanitas vanitatum*, All is vanity." . . . Atheism leads to pessimism and despair, while theism leads to faith and hope. "By their fruits you shall know them."
—EDWIN GRANT CONKLIN in *Scribner's Magazine,*
November, 1925.

Atheism Destroys Man's Nobility

I had rather believe all the fables in the Legend, and the Talmud, and the Alcoran, than that this universal frame is without a mind. And therefore God never wrought a miracle to convince atheism, because His ordinary works convince it. It is true that a little philosophy inclineth man's mind to atheism; but depth in philosophy bringeth men's minds about to religion; for while the mind of man looketh upon second causes scattered, it may sometimes rest in them, and go no farther; but when it beholdeth the chain of them confederate and linked together, it must needs fly to Providence and Deity. . . .

They that deny a God destroy man's nobility: for certainly man is of kin to the beasts by his body; and if he be not of kin to God by his spirit, he is a base and ignoble creature. . . . Man, when he resteth and assureth himself upon divine protection and favor, gathereth a force and faith, which human nature in itself could not obtain: therefore as atheism is in all

respects hateful, so in this, that it depriveth human nature of the means to exalt itself above human frailty.
—FRANCIS BACON, *Essays,* XVI: Of Atheism.

Denial of God an Act of Intellectual Suicide

The Holy Spirit tells us the "fool said in his heart there is no God." Observe the clause—"in his heart"—not in his mind, not in his reason. No, it is a rooted unwillingness to obey and love God that causes men to try and persuade themselves that no such Divine Person exists, and in this effort they too often succeed. "The wish is father to the thought," as the poet says. It is their hearts, their desires, that speak, not their reason. In the inner depths of their own consciences they know that God does and must exist, and that the universe would remain for ever a wholly and absolutely inexplicable riddle unless we accept the doctrine of an intelligent Creator—a doctrine of reason and common sense. Man cannot disguise from himself the fact—if he reflects at all—that every object around and about him proclaims the presence of God far more certainly than the human footprint on the sand proclaims the presence of man. For the traces of God's creative power are on every leaf and on every blade of grass. We cannot deny Him without dethroning reason, stultifying ourselves and committing an act of intellectual suicide—from which may God in His mercy preserve us.
—RT. REV. J. S. VAUGHAN, *Earth to Heaven*, p. 13.

SUGGESTIONS FOR STUDY AND REVIEW

1. What are the natural sources of our knowledge of God?
2. What is the nature of our knowledge of God?
3. Why can we not have a full knowledge of God?
4. Classify the arguments for the existence of God. Define the terms Teleological and Cosmological in their verbal sense.
5. What is the Law of Causality?
6. What is the basis of the Teleological argument?
7. On what facts does the Teleological argument rest?
8. Why cannot Blind Chance be the designer of the universe?
9. How does Darwinism try to explain the order and beauty so evident in the universe?

10. State and refute two objections brought against the Teleological argument.
11. Do you know any reason why God should permit pain and suffering?
12. Briefly state the Cosmological argument.
13. Why can neither Pantheism nor Materialism explain the origin of the universe?
14. Which are the Seven Riddles of the Universe?
15. Show that motion is not a property of matter.
16. Show that life must be the result of a special act of creation.
17. On what facts does the Moral argument rest?
18. What is the only explanation of these facts?
19. Why cannot Conscience be the result of education and environment?
20. On what facts is the Historical argument based?
21. What conclusion must be drawn from these facts?
22. Show why man needs God.
23. What Attributes of God can be deduced from the fact that He is a Self-existent Being?
24. Give a false and a true notion of God's omnipresence.
25. Write a brief paragraph on each of the following: *Lucretius, Epicurus, Darwin, Pasteur, Secchi, Newton, Pascal, Newman (Cardinal), Huxley, St. Columban, Nobel Prize.*

SUGGESTED READINGS

Drinkwater, F. H., *Twelve and After*, pp. 108-127.
Gerard, John, *The Old Riddle and the Newest Answer*, Chs. VII-XII.
Newman, Cardinal, *Grammar of Assent*, Ch. V.
Pallen, C. B., *As Man to Man*, pp. 66-84.
Stoddard, J. L., *Rebuilding a Lost Faith*, Chs. IV and V.

Chapter II

Man and His Place in the Universe

A. The Immortality of the Soul

1. To speak of man, says St. Augustine, is to speak of the universe. The Greeks called man the *microcosmos,* the world in miniature, because he combines in himself the elements of the universe: the gravity and extension of the mineral, the vegetative life of the plant, the sensitive life of the animal, and the intellectual life of purely spiritual beings. "What a piece of work is a man! How noble in reason! how infinite in faculty! in form, in moving, how express and admirable! in action how like an angel! in apprehension how like a god! the beauty of the world! the paragon of animals!" (Shakespeare.)

2. False notions about God necessarily lead to false notions about man. In the eyes of a Materialist, man is nothing but a highly developed brute; in the eyes of a Pantheist, every human being is a part of God, a modification of the all-embracing Divine Spirit. The Materialist, as someone has remarked, regards the earth as a menagerie; the Pantheist, as the garden of the gods.

Both of these views are wrong. Man's greatness consists in his being a creature of God, to whom God has given an immortal soul made to His own image and likeness. His littleness consists in his having been created out of nothing, and in his being related in his body to the beasts of the field.

3. False notions about man's nature lead to false notions about his destiny. When the dying man breathes his last, the Materialise says: "Now all is over. The atoms which laughed and wept in him will be used by nature to build up new bodies." If that is man's destiny, there is no meaning to his life.

4. For the Christian life is full of meaning. It is a preparation for eternity. If he plays well the part assigned to him by His Creator, he passes through the gate of death to eternal life. For the *soul of man is immortal,* and God, who made it so, will satisfy its hunger and thirst for perfect truth and goodness, joy and beauty. Hence, the immortality of the soul is, in the words of Pascal, "something which concerns us so vitally and so profoundly that one must needs be dead to every emotion before one can contemplate the thought of it with indifference."

5. Our belief in the immortality of the soul is not founded solely on Divine Revelation; it is also supported by solid philosophic and scientific arguments. These may be conveniently summarized under two heads: 1) *Arguments for the Possibility of Immortality*, and 2) *Arguments for the Fact of Immortality.*

1. The Possibility of Immortality

We do not perceive the soul directly, but, by examining the acts which proceed from it, we can learn much about its nature. This examination will show that the soul, though joined to matter, is not a material but a *spiritual substance.*

1. The Facts. a) We acquire knowledge in two ways: through the senses, and through the intellect and reason. Our five senses are our only means of knowing anything about the external world. But we know many more things than our senses tell us. We know what virtue, truth, justice, goodness, beauty are; we may have seen a good deed, heard a true statement, listened to a just judgment, contemplated a beautiful sunset; but with truth, justice, goodness, and beauty themselves we have never come in contact with our senses.

Blaise Pascal

We were told in geometry that a line is length without breadth and that a point is a position merely without size or parts. We understand these statements, and yet we have never seen or touched a geometrical line or point.

We never saw a tree that was not an oak, an elm, an ash, or some other particular tree with hundreds of characteristics that distinguish it from other particular trees, and yet we think of no particular tree when we use the word *tree*. We think of something common to all trees, but which, by itself, we have never perceived by any of our senses. When we say: "This is a tree," we mean: "This belongs to the class or species of things called trees." Our mind has, therefore, certain *ideas or notions which exist only in the mind*. These ideas are called *abstractions,* because our mind, in forming them, withdraws (abstracts) its attention from the particular or individual tree, flower, horse, etc., and considers only the class or species to which it belongs. Our senses give us pictures of the things in the external world. Our mind examines these pictures and draws from them ideas and knowledge which the senses themselves could never have given us.

Our mind can form ideas which have nothing whatever to do with material things, such as the ideas of *possibility*, *necessity*, and *obligation* represented by the words *can, must, ought*. These ideas cannot come through the senses, cannot be represented by the imagination; they pass beyond the limits of the sensible and the concrete.

b) We are conscious that our *wills are free*. We exercise our freedom many times every day in regard to things we say and do. We know that we are free to say or not to say them, to say or do them otherwise. We are free to conceal our joys and sorrows or to reveal them. No matter how strong inward or outward influences may be, we can withstand them. In the exercise of our will we know that we are not controlled by our bodies, but that we control them.

c) The human body, every particle of matter in the human body, and therefore every particle of matter in the brain, is continually changing. After a period of about seven years there is not a single brain atom of the previous period present. And yet, in spite of all these changes, each human being's personal identity remains the same from the first dawn of reason till death. We are conscious of this personal identity. We recall the past and recognize the actions done in the past, no matter how remote, as our very own.

2. Conclusion from the Facts. There is within us a power which we call intellect, reason or mind; in other words, a thinking or rational substance which we call soul. A thinking substance must be a simple spiritual substance. A simple spiritual substance is independent of matter. That which is independent of matter can exist apart from matter. That which can exist apart from matter is not involved in the dissolution of the matter to which it may be joined. Therefore the human soul can exist apart from the body to which it is joined. Being a simple substance, the soul cannot be divided into parts, and hence its existence cannot be terminated by decomposition; i.e., it cannot die or perish of itself or through the agency of any creature. God alone, who made it, can destroy it.

2. The Fact of Immortality

The soul, as we have seen, is not so absolutely dependent on the body that the dissolution of the one must necessarily involve the cessation of the other. The spirituality of the soul proves the possibility of immortality. But will the soul certainly continue to exist after the death of the body?

1. Man alone "thinks the thought of immortality." This thought moves him to the deepest depths of his being, fills him with joy and fear. How could this thought affect our souls so deeply if they were not made for eternity? If there was not in us a spark of the Divinity, how could the thought of God and of union with Him for all eternity ravish our hearts? The belief in immortality is a characteristic feature of every religion. "The thought of eternity vibrates in the soul of humanity, in the hearts of the civilized and the uncivilized races."

> It is said that the hope of immortality is an *instinct of humanity*. If so, it is surely an *instinct of man's spiritual nature* which bears witness against the testimony of the senses. The thought of immortality cannot come into the soul from the external world, where all is transitory and perishable. If in spite of the witness of nature to the contrary, the soul holds fast to the hope of immortality, the roots of this hope must be looked for in the nature of the soul itself. If no instinct in the animal kingdom is without purpose, can one of the most universal and persistent cravings of the human soul be a mere will-o'-the-wisp, a fata morgana?

Doré

The Angel of the Apocalypse Shows
St. John the Heavenly Jerusalem

2. The soul could perish only if God annihilated it.
But it is God who implanted in it the craving for eternity and
imprinted upon it the splendor of His own image. Eternal Wisdom does not destroy His works; He perfects them, guides them
to the end for which He made them. "Throughout the whole
realm of nature no substance capable of existence ever perishes. Why should the soul prove an exception to this rule?
Why should it alone suffer annihilation after a brief space of
time, when every single atom lives on? What grounds have I
for assuming that the spirit of man is a less enduring thing
than an atom of oxygen or hydrogen?"

3. Man's life here on earth is incomplete, and the more
lofty his aims, the more worthy his labors, the more incomplete will it appear to be. Even the man who lives for fame,
wealth, power, is not satisfied in this life, much less he who
lives for the ideals of truth, beauty, goodness; for he lives not

for time but for eternity; his ideals cannot be realized on this side of the grave. Unless these ideals are mocking visions, man has a right to expect the continuance of his life for its completion. (A. E. Garvie).

4. Our conscience tells us that there is a Supreme Lawgiver who will reward the good and punish the wicked. In this life the wicked often prosper and the righteous suffer. The justice of God, and our sense of justice, demand that there should be a future state in which this inequality is corrected.

Christ, Our Judge
A Sculpture on the Facade of Notre Dame, Paris

5. Emerson declares that "the impulse to seek proof of immortality is itself the strongest proof of all." We expect immortality, he argues, not merely because we desire it; but because the desire itself arises from all that is best and truest and worthiest in ourselves. The desire is reasonable, moral, social, religious; it has the same worth as the loftiest ideals and worthiest aspirations of the soul of man. The loss of the belief in immortality casts a dark shadow over the present life. "No sooner do we try to get rid of the idea of immortality—than Pessimism raises its head . . . Human griefs seem little worth assuaging; human happiness too paltry (at the best) to be worth increasing. The whole moral world is reduced to a point. Good and evil, right and wrong, become infinitesimal, ephemeral matters. The affections die away—die of their own conscious feebleness and uselessness. A moral paralysis creeps over us" (*Natural Religion*).

My own dim life should teach me this,
  That life shall live for evermore,
  Else earth is darkness at the core,
And dust and ashes all that is;

This round of green, this orb of flame,
  Fantastic beauty; such as lurks
  In some wild Poet, when he works
Without a conscience or an aim.

What then were God to such as I?
  'Twere hardly worth my while to choose
  Of things all mortal, or to use
A little patience ere I die;

'Twere best at once to sink to peace,
  Like birds the charming serpent draws,
  To drop head-foremost in the jaws
Of vacant darkness and to cease.
                    Tennyson, *In Memoriam.*

3. Objections to the Belief in Immortality

Objections to the belief in immortality have been advanced chiefly from the standpoint of *Materialism.*

1. Materialism argues that, "as life depends on a material organism, thought is a function of the brain, and the soul is but the sum of mental states, to which physical changes always correspond; therefore the dissolution of the body carries with it necessarily the cessation of consciousness." If asked for a proof that "thought is a function of the brain," the Materialist answers: "If by some accident your skull is injured, or if you lose a little of its contents, you cannot think as once you could, your memory is impaired, or you no longer give to things their proper names."

The facts are correct, but the deduction from them is false. The brain is only one of the factors of thought. Just as an instrument and an artist are necessary for the production of music, so also are brain and soul necessary for the production of thought.

Other facts adduced by Materialists in support of their theory are true only to a very limited extent. Many great men, they tell us, had large brains, whilst idiots and apes, who manifest no intellectual activity, have a small cranial capacity. The capacity of the cranial cavity of a chimpanzee is only about one-third of the normal capacity of the human brain. This, they claim, is the explanation of the vast abyss that separates the intellectual life of man from that of the ape.

We answer. The average weight of the human brain is 1,372 grams. This average has been surpassed by many of the great artists and scientists of the past. Cuvier's brain, for example, weighed 1,830, Helmholtz's 1,500, Gauss' 1,490 grams. It is a curious fact, however, that many wage-earners of very ordinary intellectual power had brains which weighed from 1,600 to 1,900 grams, whilst the brains of many great men fell far below the average. Thus the brain of Raphael weighed only 1,232, that of Leibnitz 1,257 grams. The only legitimate conclusion we can draw from brain statistics is that large and small brains are only to a very limited extent better or worse instruments of the soul.

2. Some years ago a scientist declared that the amount of *phosphorus* in the brain determines the force and energy of thought. If this is true, geese and sheep ought to be great thinkers, because their brains contain more phosphorus than any human brain.

3. Another scientist explained thought as a *"perspiration of the brain."* As the salivary gland, he says, secretes saliva, so the brain secretes thought. He suggested in all earnest that special diets should be prepared for the various kinds of intellectual activity. If this is true, if thoughts and emotions and acts of the will are nothing but material products of the brain, there must be something corporeal about them: we should be able to see them or smell them or weigh them.

4. Recent attempts to explain thought as a *chemical or electrical action in the brain* are just as far from a real solution of the mystery as the ones we have noticed above. Eliminate the idea of a spiritual force behind the 6,000,000,000 ganglion globules in the convolutions of the human brain, and no explanation is possible.

B. Man and the Lower Animals

In the Book of Genesis the creation of man is described as a twofold operation: the forming of man's body out of the slime of the earth, and the infusion of the soul into this body. Hence the question of the origin of man is also a twofold one: the origin of his body, and the origin of his soul. We shall treat them separately.

1. Origin of the Human Body. Evolutionists tell us that man was a new species sprung from some lower animal stock. The resemblances between the human body and the body of certain anthropoid (manlike) apes lend color to this theory. The differences between them are explained as due either to the slow accumulation of small variations or to a process of mutation (sudden change). The first of these alternatives is regarded by many scientists of note as positively incredible on purely scientific grounds; the second is possible, but it cannot be proved, since there is no way to register the birthdays of mutations. (Windle). "But even if the proof were forthcoming tomorrow," says Archbishop Sheehan, "that the body of the first man was evolved from the lower animals, it would not be found to contradict any solemn, ordinary, or official teaching of the Church." Does not God even now infuse the soul into organized matter at the conception of a human being?

2. Origin of the Human Soul. It has always been the teaching of the Church that each human being's soul is a special creation of God. Science has not proved, nor can it ever prove, that the spiritual, the intellectual part of man is derived from animal ancestors. The presence in man of a spiritual power which is the source of thought and reasoning, is one of the enigmas of the universe. Science cannot produce any evidence demonstrating how the vast gulf can be bridged that separates the intelligence of the most degraded race of men from the highest of the brutes. "The belief in the brute origin of his soul led Darwin to doubt if he had any right to decide, with a brain derived from that of an ape, whether there was a God or not.

Michelangelo

The Creation of Man

If he was unable to come to a decision on that point for that reason, he was equally incapable of coming to a valid conclusion on any topic whatever, and thus committed intellectual suicide." (Sir Bertram Windle).

A brief consideration of the difference between man and the highest brute will clearly show that this difference is not one of *degree* only, as evolutionists hold, but one of *kind*; in other words, that man and beast belong to two totally different orders of being.

3. Man and the Lower Animals. Two mistakes are made in treating this question: in order to establish his pet theory of the identity of animal and human nature, the evolutionist makes the animal as human as possible; in his anxiety to emphasize the difference between man and the brute, the Christian apologist does not always give the brute its due. The brute is not a human being, but it is more than a machine. It has memory and imagination; it learns new things by its own experience and can be trained by man to do very remarkable things. *What the animal lacks is intellect or reason.* It cannot form abstract ideas, cannot perceive the agreement or disagreement between two ideas, cannot draw a conclusion by the comparison of two ideas with a third. This is proved by the following facts:

a) The lower animals have never shown the faintest sign of *progress*. Animals of the same species, when in similar circumstances, always act in the same way. They seek their prey, build their nests, and care for their young in the same way. There is no individual personality about their work as there is in the work of man. Ants and bees in the time of Solomon and Homer worked as perfectly as they do now, and geese and cows were just as awkward. No animal ever made an invention; it never fashioned even the rudest weapon of defense; never lit a fire; never handed down to its offspring a useful piece of information or trick acquired from man. The crudest stone arrowhead found in some prehistoric cave or gravel-pit is regarded by all scientists as the work, not of an intelligent animal, but of a rational man.

b) The animal has *no language to express its thoughts*. Why not? Because it has no thoughts to express. "Man is man only through speech," says Wilhelm von Humboldt, "but in order to invent it he must already be man!" Animals as well as men can express feelings of pleasure and pain; some animals can be trained to utter articulate sounds; but *rational language*— i.e., the expression of thoughts, of distinct judgments, is possessed by man alone. No parrot or magpie has ever been known to combine the words it has learned from man in *new orders* so as to form other intelligible propositions.

c) Animals have *no moral notions.* Man is guided in his actions by his conscience, by his sense of right and wrong. If he acts against the dictate of his conscience he feels remorse and contrition. The animal is guided by what is pleasing to its senses and useful for the preservation of its life or the propagation of its kind. When we punish animals we do so in order to attach unpleasant recollections to the performance of certain actions, but never because we hold them *morally responsible* for their actions.

d) If the ingenuity displayed by certain lower animals is to be assigned to an intelligence similar to that of man, ants and bees, which are rated very low in the scale of life and whose brain capacity is certainly very insignificant, would be far more intelligent than the highest animals and man himself. Not even Darwin would admit such an absurdity.

4. The only conclusion from these considerations is the one drawn by the Psalmist: "What is man that Thou art mindful of him? or the son of man that Thou visitest him? Thou hast made him a little less than the Angels, Thou hast crowned him with glory and honor, Thou hast set him over the works of Thy hands. Thou hast subjected all things under his feet, all sheep and oxen, the beasts also of the fields and the birds of the air, and the fishes of the sea that pass through the paths of the sea. O Lord our Lord, how admirable is Thy name in all the earth." (*Ps.* 8).

C. Prehistoric Man

1. Since the enormous gulf that separates historic man from the lower animals may be seen by anyone who cares to look, our modern Darwinians hark back to the primitive stages of man's development in order to prove his simian ancestry. And this is the picture which they draw of prehistoric man:

He was a savage of the lowest type imaginable. At first he lived on trees like the ape, later in caves. He was ignorant of language and of fire; he ate his meat raw, his favorite dish being the marrow and brain of his fellow-savages. There was no such thing as the family. Men roamed about in hordes like deer or bisons. In the endless struggle for the possession of watering-places and hunting-grounds the strongest and trickiest survived. After an indefinite period of atheism man became a religious

animal; but his ideas of religion were very crude, originating
as they did in fear of ghosts or the spirits of the dead.

2. This picture of primitive man is not based on facts.
It is a play of the imagination, the offspring of a preconceived
theory. According to the Darwinian theory man, both body and
soul, is nothing but a more highly developed brute: hence he
must have lived at one time in a state, not of barbarism, but
of brutishness. If the facts do not square with this theory, so
much the worse for the facts.

The facts do *not* square with this theory. *Paleontology (i.e.,*
the science that treats of fossil remains of plants and animals)
and *Anthropology (i.e.,* the science that treats of the races of
men, their characteristics, origin, geographical distribution, etc.)
give a very different account of prehistoric man. Measured by
our present standards, his culture was low, but he was *human
in every respect!*

a) He invented the art of producing fire by friction—an art
not much improved upon for several thousand years, not in fact
till modern times. He roasted the flesh on which he mainly
subsisted, as is proved by the fragments of charcoal found in
the cave deposits.

b) He invented nearly all the weapons, tools, and other appli-
ances still in use today, such as the hammer, the hatchet, the
spear, the knife, the awl, and the needle. His structures, such
as huts, fences, stockades, though poor and clumsy, were in
principle the same as our own.

c) He loved and practiced art. His drawings on bone and
tusk and on the walls of caves show no mean artistic power.

> "So far as concerns the power of seizing and render-
> ing the characteristics of natural objects, some of the ear-
> liest examples of representative art in the world are among
> the best. The objects are animals, because they were the
> only ones that interested the early hunter, but tens of
> thousands of years ago the Palaeolithic cave-dwellers of
> Western France drew and carved the mammoth, the rein-
> deer, the antelope, and the horse with astonishing skill
> and spirit" (*Encyclop. Britan.*, 13th ed., Vol. 20, p. 462,
> where excellent reproductions of prehistoric pictorial art
> will be found).

d) The fossil remains quite naturally tell us little about the
religion of primitive man; still we have clear proofs that he
buried his dead reverently and believed in life after death.

D. The Age of Man

1. How long has man inhabited the earth? No one can answer this question exactly. There is the answer gathered from the dates scattered through the Bible, the answer of profane history, and the answer of the prehistoric sciences.

a) The age of the patriarchs from Adam to Moses differs, quite considerably at times, in the Hebrew text from that given in the Samaritan text and in the ancient Greek translation (the Septuagint). According to the Hebrew text there were about 4,166 years between the creation of Adam and the Birth of Christ; according to the Samaritan text 4,466 years, and according to the Septuagint 5,513 years. Which calculation is the correct one? There is no means of finding out. There may be wide gaps in the list of the patriarchs, and then several thousand years more would have to be added. Hence we are not tied down, in our interpretation of Scripture, to any definite number of years for the age of man.

b) Profane history cannot throw any more light on the age of the human race than our existing texts of the Bible. It seems certain that about the year 4000 B.C. the peoples dwelling in the valley of the Euphrates and the Tigris had developed a high degree of civilization. The history of Egypt can be traced back several hundred years more, to about the year 4200, when we find the first traces of the division of the year into 365 days.

c) Prehistoric science has nothing but guesses to offer in answer to our question. These guesses run from 1,000,000 to 25,000 years, which makes it clear that data are wanting to form even an approximate estimate of the antiquity of man.

2. But let us suppose the great antiquity of man to be rigorously proved, would there not then be a conflict between science and Divine Revelation?

We answer: Science teaches us that all men are descended from one pair. The Church teaches the same doctrine as far as the human race as it now exists is concerned. It has never made any declaration concerning the theory, occasionally put forward, that there may have been earlier races of mankind before Adam, which ceased to exist before Adam was created. Remains of the so-called Neanderthal Man have been found in various parts of the world, and yet, the race has completely and mysteriously disappeared.

The Pre-Adamite theory advanced by Giordano Bruno and the French Calvinist Peyrere in the 17th century and condemned

by the Church held that there were men not of the race of
Adam still on earth. This theory cannot be reconciled with the
Catholic doctrine of Original Sin.

3. When reading the Book of Genesis it is well to remember that the author had no intention to write *scientifically.* His
aim was to stress the *divine origin* of the world, not to give a
scientific account of the *manner in which* God carried out the
work of Creation. "Since it was not the intention of the sacred
writer to teach the inmost constitution of visible things, or the
complete order of creation, in a scientific manner, but rather
to give his countrymen a popular notion, conformable to the
ordinary language of those times and adapted to their opinions and intelligence, we must not always and regularly look
for scientific exactitude of language when interpreting this (the
first) chapter of Genesis." (Decree of the Pontifical Commission
for Biblical Studies, June 30, 1909).

<hr>

The Instinct for Beauty a
Proof of Our Immortality

We have still a thirst unquenchable. . . . This thirst belongs
to the immortality of Man. It is at once a consequence and an
indication of his perennial existence. It is the desire of the
moth for the star. It is no mere appreciation of the Beauty
before us, but a wild effort to reach the Beauty above. Inspired
by an ecstatic prescience of the glories beyond the grave, we
struggle by multiform combinations among the things and
thoughts of Time to attain a portion of that Loveliness whose
very elements perhaps appertain to eternity alone. And thus
when by Poetry, or when by Music, the most entrancing of the
poetic moods, we find ourselves melted into tears, we weep
them not through excess of pleasure, but through a certain
petulant, impatient sorrow at our inability to grasp *now,* wholly
here on earth, at once and forever, those divine and rapturous
joys of which *through* the poem, or *through* the music, we attain
to but brief and indeterminate glimpses.

—EDGAR ALLAN POE, *The Poetic Principle.*

The Soul's Testimony to its Immortality

If faith in immortality, in a future life, is an illusion, how could such an illusion have ever arisen and been believed? How comes it that we do not graze contentedly like dumb cattle on the earth, but that amidst all the bustle of life there is a restless longing in the heart of man, like the longing after a beloved home? How comes it that at all times the greatest and profoundest minds have clung to this belief, that noble natures, pure souls above all, proclaim it enthusiastically? When in the autumn and the springtime we watch the flocks of birds passing swiftly over our heads, what means the longing that draws us away to other lands? When at night we raise our eyes to the twinkling stars in the firmament, so far, so high above us, what means the swelling and straining of our heart, as though it would tear itself free from the body to seek a tearless home beyond the seas? It is the soul's testimony that we dwell in exile here, that we are destined for another, a better fatherland.

—BISHOP VON KETTELER (G. METLAKE, *Ketteler and the Christian Social Reform Movement,* Philadelphia: Dolphin Press, p. 55).

God and Our Immortal Soul

We are from our birth apparently dependent on things about us. We see and feel that we could not live or go forward without the aid of man. To a child this world is everything: he seems to himself a part of this world—a part of this world in the same sense in which a branch is part of a tree; he has little notion of his own separate and independent existence, that is, he has no just idea he has a soul. And if he goes through life with his notions unchanged, he has no just notion, even to the end of life, that he has a soul. He views himself merely in his connection with this world, which is his all; he looks to this world for his good as to an idol; and when he tries to look beyond this life, he is able to discern nothing in prospect, because he has no idea of anything, nor can fancy anything, *but* this life. And if he is obliged to fancy something, he fancies this life over again; just as the heathen, when they reflected on those traditions of another life, which were floating among them, could but fancy the happiness of the blessed to consist in the enjoyment of the sun, and the sky, and the earth, as before, only as if these were to be more splendid than they are now. . . .

Such is our state—a depending for support on the reeds, which are no stay, and overlooking our real strength—at the time when God begins His process of reclaiming us to a truer view of our place in His great system of providence. And when He visits us, then in a little while there is a stirring within us. The unprofitableness and feebleness of the things of this world are forced upon our minds; they promise but cannot perform; they disappoint us. Or, if they do perform what they promise, still (so it is) they do not satisfy us. We still crave for something, we do not well know what; but we are sure it is something which the world has not given us. And then its changes are so many, so sudden, so silent, so continual. It never leaves changing; it goes on to change, till we are quite sick at heart— then it is that our reliance on it is broken. It is plain we cannot continue to depend upon it unless we keep pace with it and go on changing too; but this we cannot do. We feel that, while it changes, we are one and the same; and thus, under God's blessing, we come to have some glimpse of the meaning of our independence of things temporal, and our immortality. And should it so happen that misfortunes come upon us (as they often do), then still more are we led to understand the nothingness of this world; then still more are we led to distrust it, and are weaned from the love of it, till at length it floats before our eyes merely as some idle veil, which, notwithstanding its many tints, cannot hide the view of what is beyond it—and we begin, by degrees, to perceive that there are but two things in the whole universe, our own soul, and the God who made it.

—NEWMAN, *Parochial and Plain Sermons*, I, p. 13ff.

The Intellectual Faculties of Man
Not Developed from Brute Instinct

The special faculties we have been discussing (i.e., the intellectual faculties) clearly point to the existence in man of something which he has not derived from his animal progenitors, something which we may best refer to as being of a spiritual essence or nature, capable of progressive development under favorable conditions. On the hypothesis of this spiritual nature, super-added to the animal nature of man, we are able to understand much that is otherwise mysterious or unintelligible in regard to him, especially the enormous influence of ideas, principles, and beliefs, over his whole life and actions. . . . Thus we may perceive that the love of truth, the delight in beauty, the passion for justice, and the thrill of exultation with which we hear of an act of courageous self-sacrifice, are the workings within us of a higher nature which has not been developed by means of the struggle for material existence.

—A. WALLACE (one of the chief exponents of Darwinism), *Darwinism,* ch. 15.

Prehistoric Man Not Inferior to Present-Day Man

When we study the quarternary fossil man, who certainly should resemble our original ancestors more than we do, we always find a man like ourselves. It is a little over ten years ago that skulls were found on the turf, in the lacustrine deposits, or in ancient caves. Scientists thought they saw in them singular characters pointing towards a savage state, incompletely developed. . . . But all such notions are vanishing. The ancient troglodytes, the cave-dwellers, the men of the turf prove to be quite a respectable society. They have heads of such proportions that many individuals now living would think themselves happy if they had heads as large. . . . And when we compare the whole of the fossil remains known until now with the present state of things we may boldly say that among the men now living there exists a much greater number of individuals relatively inferior than among the fossils in question.

—RUDOLF VIRCHOW, *Speech at the Congress of Anthropology,* Munich, 1877.

Religion and Science Are Not Incompatible

Suppose an infidel scientist, in his hatred of Christianity, would proudly refuse to accept any discovery made by a Christian scientist—the poor man would be in a sorry plight. Is he a chemist? he has to do without Berzelius, Dumas, Liebig, Deville, Chevreul, that is, about the whole of modern chemistry would have to be discovered by him. Is he a physicist? he has to prescind in electricity from the discoveries of Galvani, Volta, Ampere, Faraday, that is, from nearly everything that is known in this field. In optics, he would have to go back to the times before Fresnel, Fraunhofer, Fizeau, and would have to take up the antiquated theories of emissions; in calories, little would be left without Mayer and Joule. In astronomy, he has to renounce everything that has been discovered by Fraunhofer's telescopes.

So much about the theoretical part. But what would our

proud infidel do in active life, in industry and commerce? The unfortunate man has to sit in the dark, unless he is willing to take the old tallow candle, for stearine he owes to the Catholic Chevreul; he has to put out his electric lamps, for the electric current cannot be used without the measurements of the pious Catholics Ampère and Volta, nor can he use the electric cars. Aluminum he cannot use, as it was discovered by the Catholic Deville; in photography he is forbidden the collodium of Schoenbein; in medicine he has to do without Pelletier's quinine; the whole doctrine of microbes has to be dispensed with, as it is chiefly due to the Catholic Pasteur. And in numberless other cases he would be thrown back into a condition which we would call intolerable, if he disdained to use what he ultimately owes to the genius of scientists who were sincere Christians.

> —KARL A. KNELLER, S.J., *Christianity and the Leaders of Modern Science,* St. Louis: B. Herder Book Co.

Some Modern Scientists on the Supposed Antagonism between Science and Faith

Nothing is more unfounded than the objection made by some well-meaning but undiscerning persons, that the study of natural science induces a doubt of religion and the immortality of the soul. Be assured that its logical effect upon any well-ordered mind must be just the opposite.

> —The Astronomer JOHN HERSCHEL (d. 1871), *Preliminary Discourse on the Study of Natural Philosophy,* p. 7.

Of Karl Friedrich *Gauss* (d. 1855), the greatest mathematician of the 19th century, his biographer says: "The conviction of a personal existence after death, the firm belief in an ultimate Ruler of things, in an eternal, just, all-wise and all-powerful God, formed the foundation of his religious life, which, with his unsurpassed scientific researches, resolved itself into a perfect harmony."

> —J. DONAT, S.J., *The Freedom of Science,* New York: Joseph F. Wagner, Inc., p. 210.

Andre Marie *Ampère* (d. 1836), the celebrated investigator in the field of electricity, after passing through torturing doubts, regained undisturbed possession of his Catholic faith, and was a pious son of the Church at the time of his brilliant discoveries. He had frequent intercourse with Frederick Ozanam, and the conversation would always turn to God. Ampère would cover his forehead with his hands, exclaiming: "How great is God, Ozanam! how great is God, and our knowledge is as nothing!" He knew the *Imitation of Christ* by heart.

—J. Donat, S.J., op. *cit.,* p. 212.

Michael *Faraday* (d. 1867), perhaps the greatest experimentist of all time, wrote to a lady: "I belong to a small and despised Christian sect, known by the name of Sandemanians. Our hope is based upon the belief which is in Christ." In 1847 he concluded his lectures in the Royal Institution with the following words: "In teaching us those things, our science should prompt us to think of Him whose works they are."

—JONES, *Life and Letters of Faraday.*

Louis *Pasteur* (d. 1895), the discoverer of various bacteria, was to his death a staunch Catholic. "As his soul departed, he held in his hands a small crucifix of brass, and his last words were acts of Faith and Hope." When one of his pupils asked him how he could be so religious after all his thinking and studying, he replied: "Just because I have thought and studied, I have remained religious like a peasant of Brittany, and had I thought and studied still more, I would be as religious as a peasant woman of Brittany."

—*Revue des Questions Scientifiques,* 1896, p. 385.

Theism in natural science, or, if you prefer, in natural philosophy, rests upon the basis of a fundamental view which an old formula has clothed in words as simple as they are sublime: "I believe in God, the Almighty Creator of Heaven and of Earth." This confession does not cling to theistic scientists like an egg-shell from the time of unsophisticated childhood faith; it is the result of their entire scientific thought and judgment. This conviction has been professed by the most discerning natural scientists of all ages.

—J. Reinke, *Naturwissenschaft und Religion.*

Evolution, a Theory, Not a Law

The term "evolution" may be used in many senses. It may signify development in its most general acceptation. It may signify the development of the individual body from the condition of the fertilized cell into the mature structure which characterizes a particular species. It may signify the development of individual members of a species from one degree of perfection to another. It may signify *the hypothesis that all the specific forms of life which we see in the world today have developed from some form or forms, unicellular or multicellular, through countless changes into their present condition.* It is evolution in the last sense that is the subject of so much controversy today. In this sense it *is* often called "transformism." In as much as it owes its present vogue to Darwin's presentation of it, transformism is often called Darwinism. But Darwin did not originate the evolutionary hypothesis. His contribution consisted in the enunciation of the "laws" which, he assumed, determined the course of evolution, and in the assembling of the facts to support the hypothesis.

Evolution may be *materialistic* or *theistic*: materialistic, when the world is regarded as self-existing; theistic, when the world is regarded as having been created by God.

Materialists, who refuse to regard the human soul as a spiritual, substantial principle, include the human, as well as the animal, mind within the scope of evolution.

Theistic evolutionists who recognize the human soul as a spiritual, substantial principle, exclude it from the scope of evolution.

That theistic evolution, as applied to merely vegetative and sentient life, is absolutely possible, is evident from the fact that it involves no contradiction in terms. The Infinite Cause can produce any effect which does not involve self-contradiction.

Is transformism a law of nature? That is a law of nature which is a constantly recurring phenomenon of nature. Is the transformation of living bodies from species to species a constantly recurring phenomenon of nature?

Evolutionists are justified in making the *assumption* that all life is subject to the law of transformism. But though, for the sake of investigation, they may assume the truth of the universal proposition, *they may not assume that the facts support this assumption.* They must establish the particular facts. And where are the established facts which show that transformism did actually occur in the past? The earth as the burial ground of the dead animals of ages past is eloquent of death. It is silent about their origin. The investigator may infer as much as he chooses. But inference is not evidence. Everybody can appreciate evidence, and must assent to the truth which it establishes. Mere inferences, apart from evidence, may be formed at will and do not compel assent. When evolutionists supply the evidence which is necessary to support their assumption, the world will assent to the truth of it because evidence compels assent. When that happens, if it ever does, evolution will be no more discussed than is the rotation of the earth.

—JOHN X. PYNE, S.J., *The Mind,* New York: Benziger Brothers, p. 7 ff.

The Theory of Evolution Not Opposed to Religious Truths

In itself the theory of evolution, which asserts the variability of species of animals and plants, is by no means opposed to religious truths. It neither includes a necessity of assuming the origin of the human soul from the essentially lower animal soul, nor is it an atheistic theory. On the contrary, such an evolution would most clearly testify to God's wisdom in laying such a wonderful basis for the progress of nature, provided this theory could be proved by scientific facts; indeed, for an evolution within narrow limits, circumstantial evidence is not lacking.

That there is no contradiction between the theory of evolution and the fundamental tenets of the Christian Creed is sufficiently shown by the representatives of the theory. Lamarck and Saint-Hilaire, both of them representatives of the theory of evolution long before Darwin, believed in God. There were, prior to Darwin, two celebrated Catholic scientists, Ampère and d'Omalius, who had decidedly taken the part of Saint-Hilaire in his controversy with Cuvier. And also after Darwin, a number of Christian and Catholic scientists have contended for the theory of evolution, as, for instance, the Swiss geologist Heer; also Quenstedt, Volkmann, and the American geologist Lyell. More recently Catholic scientists have expressed themselves in favor of the theory of evolution; for instance, the noted zoologist Erich Wasmann, S.J., and the geologists Waagen and Lossen.

—J. DONAT, S. J., *The Freedom of Science,* p. 223.

Referring to jubilant anti-evolutionist cries that arise from time to time in certain quarters, the late Sir Bertram Windle issued a warning which cannot be too often repeated: "Such anti-evolutionary cries should never, under any circumstances, come from the Catholic ranks. Of all people we can afford to survey this scene of conflict with complete calm, for we know that God's two books of revelation and nature cannot possibly contradict each other. Hence, as Leo XIII told us, and as common sense dictates, we should rejoice in any new discovery, whether it tells for or against evolution; for the truth is what we are looking for, and not victory over our supposed antagonists. The fact is, that this exultation on the part of anti-evolutionists leads their opponents very naturally and logically to conclude that these would-be defenders of religion believe that the establishment of evolution as a fact would mean the destruction of the Christian faith, whereas nothing could be more untrue or more ridiculous."

—*Fortnightly Review,* Oct. 1931, p. 235.

SUGGESTIONS FOR STUDY AND REVIEW

1. What is man according to the Pantheist? According to the Materialist?
2. In what does the greatness and littleness of man consist?
3. What facts prove that the human soul is a spiritual substance?
4. What follows from the spirituality of the soul?
5. Give three proofs for the fact of immortality.
6. What objections does Materialism raise against the immortality of the soul?
7. Briefly refute each objection.
8. What does the Book of Genesis say about the creation of man?
9. Is the theory that the *body* of the first man was evolved from the lower animals condemned by the Church? Why can this theory never be proved?
10. What must we hold in regard to the origin of the soul?
11. Give four proofs to show that the lower animals have no intellect or reason.
12. Show that Prehistoric man was truly human in every respect.
13. What do we know about the age of the human race from the Bible? From profane history? From the Prehistoric sciences?
14. Briefly discuss the Pre-Adamite theory.
15. What should we bear in mind when reading the first chapter of the Book of Genesis?

16. Annotate the following: *Cuvier, Helmholtz, Gauss, Leibnitz. Raphael, Septuagint, Giordano Bruno, Emerson, Tennyson.*

SUGGESTED READINGS

Hill, M. P., *The Catholic's Ready Answer*, pp. 207-216.
Kneller, C. A., *Christianity and the Leaders of Modern Science.*
Pesch, T., *The Christian Philosophy of Life*, pp. 71-114.
Stoddard, J. L., *Rebuilding a Lost Faith*, Ch. VI.
Windle, Sir Bertram, *The Catholic Church and Its Reaction with Science*, Chs. X and XI.

Schleibner

"Wherefore having the loins of your mind girt up, being sober, trust perfectly in the grace which is offered you in the revelations of Jesus Christ." (*1 Peter* 1:13)

Section II

Reasonableness of
Our Belief in Christ

Chapter I

Revelation and the
Signs of Revelation

1. God Reveals Himself in Many Ways. The contemplation of the universe, of nature and the human soul, lifts our thoughts up to God, but it does not bring the living God down to us. Whether He wishes to reveal Himself to us only from afar through the works of His power, or whether He wishes to incline Himself personally to us, we can find out only from God Himself.

It is true, God has always been near to His creatures, especially to the understanding and the heart of His rational creatures. "We are distinct from God, but there is nothing nearer to us than God. Apart from Divine Being nothing exists; apart from Divine activity nothing moves; without Divine light there is no knowledge; without Divine love no heart can love." St. Paul sums up this intimate relationship of God to us in the three words: "In Him we *live*, and *move*, and *are*."

God is also near to us in another way: by the wonders of His Grace. He enlightens our understanding and moves our will to do good and to avoid evil.

2. Revelation. But neither God's Providence over all creation nor the mysterious workings of His grace in the souls of men, is a *personal revelation* of Himself, a drawing back of the veil or curtain which conceals Him from us, a discovering of Himself to us.

It is only when God takes one of us into His confidence and gives him a message for his fellow-men, that we can speak of Supernatural Revelation, of Revelation in the strict sense of the word.

49

There are also *private revelations* made by God for the benefit of one or a few individuals. We are speaking here of *public revelation* made for all mankind.

3. We need not stop to prove the possibility of Revelation. God, who gave to men the power to communicate with one another, can, if He so wills, communicate with men. The *probability* that He did make a revelation is evident from the consideration of the unhappy condition of man and the goodness and mercy of God.

> "Revelation," says Cardinal Newman, "comes to you recommended and urged upon you by the most favorable anticipations of reason. The very difficulties of nature make it likely that a Revelation should be made; the very mysteries of creation call for some act on the part of the Creator, by which those mysteries shall be alleviated to you or compensated. You cannot help expecting it from the hands of the All-merciful, unworthy as you feel yourselves of it. It is not that you can claim it, but that He inspires the hope of it; it is not that you are worthy of the gift, but it is the gift which is worthy of your Creator. The very fact that here is a Creator, and a hidden one, powerfully bears you on, and sets you down at the

Plato

very threshold of a Revelation, and leaves you there, looking up earnestly for Divine tokens that a Revelation has been made."

Such a Divine Revelation was ardently looked forward to by many of the noblest minds of antiquity. Plato used to long for the day which would bring with it a guide to instruct us how to conduct ourselves towards God and our fellow-men. "No man is in a condition to help himself," says Seneca; "someone above him must stretch forth his hand and raise him up."

If man was destined to a *supernatural end*—i.e., to the vision of God—a *supernatural revelation,* was absolutely *necessary,* for his unaided reason will never tell him that.

4. Credentials of Revelation. All founders of religions in ancient and modern times claimed to be messengers of God commissioned to make known His will and truth to men. But were they really sent by God? Did they have the proper *credentials*? Could they prove that the Spirit of God spoke through them? This is the all-important question.

To prove that a man is the mouthpiece of God, it is not sufficient to point to the edifying and pious character of his teaching. However, we can confidently assert that *a writing whose doctrine conflicts with right reason and morality cannot be a revelation from the all-holy and all-wise God.*

5. Miracles and Prophecies are the only infallible credentials which God gives His messengers. If God puts His own miraculous power at the disposal of a teacher, or permits him to look into the secrets of the future, we can say without hesitation or fear of error that that teacher has been sent by God.

Miracles are extraordinary works which cannot be done by the powers of nature, but only through the omnipotence of God. Anyone who admits the existence of a personal God, the Creator of all things, must admit the *possibility of miracles*; for He who fixed the course of nature can alter, suspend, or supersede it at His pleasure.

In order to decide whether a miracle has taken place or not, two things are necessary: 1) the fact itself—e.g., the raising of a dead person to life—must be clearly established, and 2) every possible natural explanation of the event must be excluded.

We do not know everything that the forces of nature can do, but we certainly do know some things that they can never do. We know, for example, that natural forces alone will never raise to life a man who has been really dead, or restore a missing member of the human body, or instantaneously cure a wound or a fracture. The question of miracles is, in a word, a question of evidence.

A *Prophecy* is a foretelling of a future event, which God alone could know because it depends either on the free will of God or the free will of man. A true prophecy must 1) be made before the event; 2) it must be definite, not ambiguous or obscure; 3) the event predicted must be of such a nature as to be beyond the possibility of guess or human prevision.

A prophecy, if fulfilled, is just as conclusive a proof of Divine authority as a miracle: a miracle is possible only because God is omnipotent, a prophecy because He is omniscient.

If, then, the doctrine taught by one who claims to be sent by God to speak in His name to the whole human race is noble, elevating, in harmony with reason, satisfying to human aspirations, and beneficial to society; if this doctrine is confirmed by evident miracles and prophecies; and if it gains such a firm hold on the minds and hearts of men as to work a moral revolution in the world—the teacher has made good his claim. He is a messenger of God and his doctrine is divine.

6. Jesus Christ claimed to be not only a messenger of God, but the Son of God Himself. He supported His claim by the purity and sublimity of His teaching, by the holiness of His life, by numerous miracles during his lifetime, and by the crowning miracle of His resurrection. Within an incredibly short space of time His doctrine, linked as it was with so many sacrifices, spread far and wide. These are the grounds on which the noblest of mankind have been content to base their faith in the Divinity of Christ and the Christian Religion. Before we examine them in detail we must first establish the historical value of the sources from which we derive our knowledge of Christ and His teaching.

SUPPLEMENTARY READING

There Must Be Mysteries in a Revealed Religion

No revelation can be complete and systematic, from the weakness of the human intellect; *so far as it is not such, it is mysterious.* When nothing is revealed, nothing is known, and there is nothing to contemplate or marvel at; but when something is revealed, and only something, there are forthwith difficulties and perplexities. A revelation is a religious doctrine viewed on its illuminated side; a mystery is the selfsame doctrine viewed on the side unilluminated. Thus religious truth is neither light nor darkness, but both together; it is like the dim view of a country seen in the twilight, with forms half extricated from the darkness, with broken lines and isolated masses.

—Newman, *Essays, Critical and Historical*

Necessity of Creeds and Dogmas

I myself am totally incapable of comprehending what a religion is which is free from creeds and dogmas. A creed is a formal statement of something you believe. A dogma is a particular proposition stating a belief. How can you teach anything religious or irreligious, sacred or secular, which shall not have in it something in the nature of creed and dogma—that is to say, definite propositions embodying what are believed to be definite principles? If it were possible to teach religion without creed and dogma, religion would be different from every other subject of education, the whole of which consists of definite propositions and definite beliefs.   —ARTHUR BALFOUR

SUGGESTIONS FOR STUDY AND REVIEW

1. Show that God reveals Himself to us in many ways.
2. When can we speak of supernatural revelation in the strict sense of the word?
3. What is a private revelation?
4. Show that revelation is possible and probable.
5. In what case would a supernatural revelation be absolutely necessary? Why?
6. What are the infallible credentials of God's messengers?
7. What are miracles?
8. Why do we say that the question of miracles is a question of evidence?
9. Refute the objection: "We do not know all the powers of nature, therefore we cannot tell whether a true miracle has ever happened."

10. What are prophecies?
11. What are the marks of a true prophecy?
12. Show that miracles and prophecies are conclusive proofs of divine authority.

SUGGESTED READINGS

Joyce, G. H., *The Question of Miracles*, pp. 1-42.
Newman, Cardinal, *Grammar of Assent*, pp. 384 ff.
Apologia, pp. 241-246.
Pesch, T., *Christian Philosophy of Life*, pp. 142-149.
Stoddard, J. L., *Rebuilding a Lost Faith*, Chs. VII and XVIII.

The Good Shepherd
Fresco in a Roman Catacomb
(A.D. 250)

Portrait of Christ
Cemetery of St. Domitilla
(A.D. 400)

Another Portrait of Christ as the Good Shepherd
A mosaic in the mausoleum of Galla Placidia (A.D. 450)

CHAPTER II

Sources of Our Knowledge of Christ and His Teaching

A. Non-Christian Sources

History knows only *one* Teacher of the Christian Faith and Founder of the Christian Church: *Jesus of Nazareth*, who was born in Bethlehem during the reign of the Emperor Augustus and was crucified about 33 years later under the Emperor Tiberius. Less than a hundred years after His death and resurrection the spiritual kingdom which He founded was spread all over the then known world.

1. We can easily see why the non-Christian contemporaries of the first Christians had very little to say about Christ and Christianity. Both Jews and pagans despised a religion whose founder had died the shameful death of the cross. Such a religion was, in the words of its greatest preacher, "unto the Jews a stumbling-block, and unto the Gentiles foolishness." Still both Jewish and pagan writers have recorded enough to prove the absurdity of the claim set up in recent times by certain enemies of the Christian religion, that Christ was a mere myth, not an historical personage.

2. Tacitus, the greatest of the Roman historians, bears clearest testimony 1) to the founding of Christianity by Christ; 2) to the death of Christ under Pontius Pilate; 3) to the rapid spread of Christianity and the attempt of Nero to extirpate it.

> "Nero," he writes, "to put an end to the common talk that Rome had been set on fire by his order, imputed it to others, visiting with a refinement of punishment those detestable criminals who went by the name of Christians. *The author of that denomination was Christus, who had been executed in Tiberius's time by the Procurator Pontius Pilate.* The pestilent superstition, checked for a while, burst out again, not only throughout Judea ... but throughout the city of Rome also." (*Annal.* XV, 44).

3. Pliny the Younger, sent in A.D. 111 by the Emperor Trajan as Propraetor into Bithynia, is startled and perplexed, as he tells the Emperor, by the number, influence, and pertinacity of the Christians whom he finds there and in the neighboring province of Pontus. The temples of the gods were almost forsaken and purchasers of victims for the sacrifices were most rare to find. Curious to know something more definite about the Christians, he is informed that nothing can compel a real Christian to invoke the gods or to offer wine and incense to the Emperor's image. The whole of their crime was that "they were accustomed to assemble on a stated day before dawn and to *sing together a hymn to Christ as God,* and to bind themselves by an oath, not to any crime, but on the contrary to keep from theft, robbery, breach of promise, and appropriating deposits" (*Eph.* 97).

4. Suetonius, the biographer of the Caesars, regarded the Christians as a Jewish sect. Speaking of the expulsion of the Jews from Rome under the Emperor Claudius (A.D. 51 or 52), he says they were driven out "because they were making continual disturbances under the *instigation of Christus.*" Evidently Suetonius believed that Christ was in Rome under the Emperor Claudius. His mention of Christ may have reference to differences between Jews and Christians.

5. The Jewish historian Flavius Josephus (A.D. 37-100) speaks of Christ in two places of his *Jewish Antiquities.* In Book XVIII, 3,2, he writes:

> "At this time appeared Jesus, a wise man, if it be right to call him a man, for he worked miracles. He was the teacher of men who received the truth with joy, and He drew after Him many Jews and many Greeks. He was the Christ. On the denunciation of the first men of our nation, Pilate condemned Him to the cross; but those who loved Him from the beginning did not cease to love Him. For He appeared to them risen on the third day, as the divine prophets had foretold concerning Him, as also a thousand other marvels about Him. The sect which receives from Him the name of Christians exists even to this day."
>
> There is also a brief mention of Christ in Book XX, 9,1: "Ananus (A.D. 62) summoned the Great Council and set before it James, the brother of *Jesus who is called the Christ*, and some others, and had them condemned to be stoned to death."

6. The Talmud contains twelve references to Christ. All of them are filled with hatred of the very name of Jesus. Christ's miracles are not denied but ascribed to magical arts which He had brought from Egypt. His death by crucifixion is placed "on the eve of the Feast of the Passover."

7. In a letter of exhortation addressed by a certain Syrian named **Mara** to his son Serapion (between A.D. 73 and 160) Christ is called the "wise king of the Jews" who was murdered by His own people. "What did it profit the Jews," asks Mara, "to put their wise king to death, seeing that from that time on the kingdom was taken from them?"

B. CHRISTIAN SOURCES

1. The Epistles of St. Paul and the Other Apostles

As Christian sources of our knowledge of Christ and His teaching we have, first of all, the **Epistles of St. Paul.**

1. Very few Biblical scholars even of the extreme Rationalist school question the historical character of the principal Epistles of St. Paul. Harnack and Juelicher, the acknowledged leaders among the modern Rationalists, admit without hesitation that the Epistles to the Thessalonians, Galatians, Corinthians, Romans, and Philippians were written by St. Paul about A.D. 49-59 or A.D. 53-64.

Saint Paul

2. It is a disputed question whether St. Paul knew Jesus personally. At all events the details of His life were well known to him. He reminds the Galatians (3,1) that he had "set forth before their eyes Jesus Christ Crucified." He was acquainted with the particulars of the passion and death of Christ (*1 Cor.* 2). He speaks of His birth, of His descent from David, of His

Dürer

Saints John, Peter, Mark and Paul

absolute sinlessness, of His unselfishness and obedience unto
death. The Resurrection is the central theme of his preaching.
He even mentions several apparitions of the risen Lord which
are not recorded in the Gospels. His whole life was patterned
on that of Christ, and he could say to the faithful: "Be ye followers of me, as I am of Christ."

3. The Epistles written by the other Apostles contain
very few direct references to the life of Christ. *St. Peter* mentions the death of Christ, His descent into Limbo, His resurrection, ascension, and promised second coming (*1 Peter* 3:18-22).
Like St. Paul he exhorts the faithful to follow in the footsteps
of Christ. (*1 Peter* 2:21).

In his *First Epistle, St. John* speaks of his personal experience of the Incarnate Word: "That which was from the beginning, that which we have heard, that which we have seen with
our eyes, that which we beheld, and our hands handled, in
regard of the Word of Life . . . we declare to you also, in order
that you may have fellowship with us." (*1 John* 1:1-4).

All the Epistles presuppose that those to whom they are addressed already possessed a thorough knowledge of the life and
teaching of Christ.

2. The Four Gospels

The most important sources of our knowledge of the teaching and history of Christ are the Four Gospels. To prove the
existence of Christian Revelation, it is sufficient to prove the
historical authority of the Gospels.

**There are three tests by which the historical author-
ity of a work can be established: its genuineness, its
integrity, and its veracity;** in other words, if it be the work
of the author to whom it is ascribed; if the text be substantially as it left the author's hand; if it be shown that the author
himself was well-informed and truthful.

The Gospels of Sts. Matthew, Mark, Luke, and John satisfy
these three tests, and we can therefore accept them unhesitatingly as historical; i.e., as faithful narratives of past events.

The word *Gospel* means glad tidings or good news concerning Christ, the kingdom of God, and salvation. "And Jesus went
about all Galilee, teaching in the Synagogues, and preaching the
Gospel of the Kingdom" (*Matt.* 4:23). Hence the word was very
properly applied to the history of the life and teachings of Christ.
The writers of the Gospels are called Evangelists, from the Greek

word for good news—*euangelion.* The Gospels of Matthew, Mark, and Luke are called the Synoptic Gospels, as distinguished from the Fourth, because of their many agreements in matter, arrangement, and language (Greek, *sunopsis,* presenting or taking a common view of anything). The problem as to the origin and the relations of the Synoptic Gospels presented by their resemblances, is known as the *Synoptic Problem.*

a) THE GOSPELS ARE GENUINE

The genuineness (as well as the integrity and historical trustworthiness) of a work may be proved by *extrinsic arguments*—that is, by the testimony of writers who lived about the same time—or by *intrinsic* arguments drawn from the style and contents of the book itself.

Extrinsic arguments give us historical certitude of the genuineness of a book, if it is clear that the witnesses are trustworthy, and that their testimony has not been falsified.

Intrinsic arguments do not, in many cases, sufficiently determine the author and the exact time of composition. They are very useful, however, as confirmations of the external proofs.

I. Extrinsic Arguments

1. Our four Gospels existed in the earliest days of the Church.

a) The *Didache,* (i.e., the Doctrine of the Twelve Apostles, written between A.D. 80 and 100) quotes passages from Matthew and Luke. The Our Father, which is cited according to the text of St. Matthew, is introduced with the words: "As the Lord commands in His Gospels."

b) The *Epistle of Clement to the Corinthians* (about A.D. 96) contains ten texts taken from the Gospels of Matthew and Mark.

c) The *Epistle attributed to St. Barnabas* (about A.D. 100-130) contains many allusions to Matthew and several to Mark and Luke.

d) *St. Ignatius of Antioch* (martyred A.D. 107) quotes Matthew, Luke and John in his seven *Epistles.*

Thus we see that about the year 100 the first three Gospels were in existence; shortly afterwards the Fourth Gospel is also known.

e) The *Heretics* of the earliest times were well acquainted with our Gospels. In the first half of the second century the Gnostics

The Four Evangelists

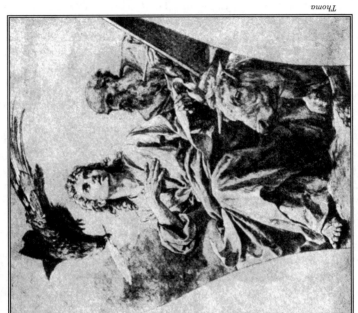

Thoma

Sts. John and Luke

Thoma

Sts. Matthew and Mark

made use of them. *Marcion* (about A.D. 140), whom Justin and Tertullian regarded as the most dangerous of all heretics, built up his new sect on the Gospel of St. Luke and the Epistles of St. Paul; but he also made use of Matthew and John.

2. The authors of the Gospels are Apostles and Disciples of the Apostles.

When there was question of choosing a successor to Judas, all agreed with St. Peter that he must be one who had been with Jesus "from the Baptism of John until the Ascension," because only such a man could be a trustworthy witness of the life of Christ. The early Church was equally strict in her demands in regard to her sacred books. They were regarded as trustworthy only if they were written directly or indirectly by Apostles. Besides the carefully guarded tradition of the Church we have the direct testimony of ecclesiastical writers of the earliest times that our Gospels were really the work of Matthew, Mark, Luke, and John; that is, of two Apostles and two companions and disciples of Apostles.

a) *Papias,* Bishop of Hierapolis in Phrygia (about A.D. 130), who was a disciple of St. John, friend of St. Polycarp, and master of St. Irenus, mentions the Gospels of St. Matthew and St. Mark:

"*Mark* neither heard the Lord nor followed Him; but subsequently, as I said, attached himself to Peter, who used to frame his teaching to meet the immediate wants of his hearers, and not as making a connected narrative of the Lord's discourses . . .

"*Matthew* wrote the *logia* (i.e., a record of the words and works of Our Lord) in the Hebrew language, and they translated them to the best of their ability."

b) *St. Justin Martyr* (about A.D. 150) narrates that the Gospels were read at the meetings of the Christians. In another place he says that the Gospels were written by Apostles and disciples. He quotes about twenty verses from the Sermon on the Mount, refers to Messianic prophecies contained in the Gospel of St. Matthew, and describes the Annunciation and many incidents of the birth of Christ found in St. Luke.

c) Within twenty years of the death of Justin, *Tatian,* who had been a pupil of Justin, produced a continuous narration of the Gospel-history which received the name *Diatesseron* ("through four"). It is in the main a compilation from our four Gospels.

d) *St. Irenaeus* (about A.D. 180), a friend of St. Polycarp, who, as we know, was a disciple of St. John, mentions the authors of the four Gospels:

> "*Matthew* published his Gospel among the Hebrews in
> their own tongue, whilst Peter and Paul were preaching
> and founding the Church in Rome. After their departure
> *Mark,* the disciple and interpreter of Peter, handed down
> in writing to us those things which Peter had preached;
> and *Luke,* the attendant of Paul, wrote in a book the
> Gospel which Paul had preached. Afterwards *John,* the
> disciple of the Lord, who also reclined on His bosom, pub-
> lished his Gospel while staying at Ephesus in Asia" (*Adver-
> sus Haereses*, III, 1, 1).

e) *Tertullian* (about A.D. 200) regarded the claim to be beyond
controversy that the four Gospels had been in the possession
of the Church since the time of the Apostles; "Matthew and
John being Apostles, Mark and Luke disciples of Apostles"
(*Adversus Marcionem*, IV, 2 and 5).

f) *Origen* (born about A.D. 183, died A.D. 253) in Egypt hears
the same testimony as Tertullian in Africa and Irenaeus in
Asia. He names the four evangelists in the same order as we
have them now as the authors of the four Gospels, and says
that these four are the only Gospels approved by the Church.

From these testimonies it is clear that the four Gospels were
in use at the end of the second century in Churches far apart,
and that their genuineness was acknowledged by Catholics and
heretics alike. "Probably there is not one of the pagan classics,"
Archbishop Sheehan justly remarks, "whose genuineness can
be supported by such convincing evidence. No one disputes that
Caesar was the author of the *Commentaries on the Gallic Wars*,
and yet the only ancient references to the work are found,
about one hundred years after its composition, in the writings
of Plutarch and Suetonius."

2. Internal Evidence

**What does a careful examination of the Gospels them-
selves tell us about their authors and the time of their
composition?**

1. The Gospels are written in Hellenistic Greek, a form of
the Greek language strongly marked by Hebrew phrases and
idioms, and employed by Jewish writers, such as Philo and
Josephus, as a literary medium during the first century after
Christ, but not later.

2. The style of the Gospels is vivid and colorful; only men
who were themselves witnesses of the events related could

have described them in such a manner.

> "The Gospels," says Harnack, "stand in marked con-
> trast to the literature of all succeeding ages. This liter-
> ary type, this simple and impressive form of narration,
> could not be reproduced by writers of a later date. It is
> evident that we have in the Gospels a genuine product
> of the time which they describe."

3. In the middle of the 19th century a school of critics, known
as the Tuebingen School, tried to show that our Gospels were
composed well on in the second century. Those theories are now
discredited. "With regard to the first three Gospels it may be
confidently asserted that the local coloring in them is predomi-
nantly Palestinian, and that they show no sign of acquaintance
with questions and circumstances of the second century; and
that the fourth Gospel is not such as to justify its being placed,
at furthest, much after the beginning of that century" (V. H.
Stanton in the *Encyclop. Britan.*, Art. "Gospels").

4. Those who try to fix the date of the composition of the
Synoptic Gospels later than the year 70 A.D. do not do so for
any plausible reasons, but solely because they find the prophecy
of the ruin of the city and the temple recorded in them; and
as they proclaim the impossibility of all prophecy, they have
to declare that this prophecy was written *after* the event. The
fact, however, that the prophecy of the destruction of Jerusalem
is associated in the Gospels with the prophecy of the end of
the world, proves beyond a doubt that it was written down
before the year 70. St. Matthew, who always lays special stress
on the fulfillment of prophecies, would not have overlooked
the fulfillment of Christ's great prediction if it had already
taken place.

b) The Gospels Are Intact

**Even the most radical opponents of Christianity admit
that the Gospels have come down to us substantially intact;
that is, free from any grave alterations and additions.**

1. We know from St. Justin that from the very beginning
the Gospels were read at public worship. The value of this
"guarantee of publicity" may be measured by the following incidents: Bishop Spiridion openly rebuked a fellow-bishop who, in
quoting a Scripture text, substituted another word having the
same meaning as the original, but which appeared more

elegant. St. Jerome could with difficulty be prevailed upon by Pope Damasus to revise the old Latin translation of the Bible, for fear of being regarded by the people as a corrupter of the Sacred Text. And this fear of St. Jerome was not groundless. "A bishop of our province," St. Augustine wrote to him, "having begun to read your translation of the Bible in his church, came to a passage of the prophet Jonas, which you have translated differently from what was known to the memory and ears of everyone, and sung during many generations. Thereupon a great tumult arose among the people, caused principally by the Greeks, who called out that the text was falsified. . . . The bishop, not to remain without a flock, after this great danger, was obliged to correct the passage as if it was a fault."

2. There are, it is true, many different *readings (variants,* as they are called) in the hundreds of ancient manuscripts of the Gospels that have come down to us, but they prove nothing against the integrity of the Gospels. As they leave untouched the essential parts of every sentence, it is clear that they are due solely to errors of copyists or translators, and that the idea of introducing any *real changes* into the text had never occurred to anyone as at all possible in such a book.

3. An Objection Answered. But, it may be objected, does not the earliest existing manuscript of the New Testament date only from the fourth century? Isn't it therefore possible that any number of changes may have been introduced into the Gospel text during the preceding centuries?

We answer: Besides the earliest Greek manuscript, the *Codex Vaticanus* referred to in the objection, we possess other manuscripts nearly as old and not copied from the *Codex Vaticanus;* viz., the *Codex Alexandrinus*, the *Codex Sinaiticus*, and the *Codex of St. Ephrem.* All these manuscripts agree substantially with one another. They also agree with the numerous quotations contained in the writings of the early Fathers of the Church, and with the oldest translation of the Gospels, such as the Syrian, which dates from the middle of the second century, and the Latin, which was already old when Tertullian wrote towards the end of the second century. Hence it is clear that, although we no longer possess the original manuscripts of the Evangelists themselves, the Gospels have remained substantially such as they were written at the beginning.

The earliest manuscript of Horace dates from the 7th century, of Cicero from the 9th, of Euripides from the

CODICES OF THE BIBLE

Codex Vaticanus,
4th century

Codex Sinaiticus,
4th century

Codex Alexandrinus,
5th century

Codex of St. Ephrem,
5th century

13th, and yet no one doubts that these manuscripts are substantially the unaltered descendants of the originals.

The Christian Gospels are thus in a far stronger position than the Greek and Roman classics, and no one would ever have thought of questioning their integrity, but for the fact that they report miracles and prophecies and contain a Divine law of belief and conduct against which the Rationalist and the irreligious of every description rebel. At the present day all critics of note, as we have said, allow that there was no substantial alteration of the text of the Gospels. In regard to miracles, they admit that apparently miraculous events do occur, but that these can be explained by natural causes. How the great miracles of Christ—e.g., the resurrection of Lazarus, His own resurrection, the multiplication of the loaves, etc.—can be explained by natural causes, they do not tell us; they simply ask us to take their word for it, that a natural explanation will some day be found.

C) The Gospels Are Truthful

Our Gospels are trustworthy in the highest degree. This will be clear from the following considerations:

1. The authors knew the facts. Two of them, Matthew and John, had been companions of Christ; the other two, Mark and Luke, were disciples of the Apostles and lived in constant intercourse with them.

The facts which they record were recent, striking, often extraordinary and miraculous, and therefore calculated to attract attention. Christ spoke openly for the most part and performed His miracles in full daylight, and frequently under the very eyes of His enemies, who did not deny them, but tried to explain them away by attributing them to the power of the devil.

No one will say that the authors of the Gospels were simpletons, or the victims of hallucination. How could simpletons have spread the teaching of Christ among all classes of Jewish, Greek, and Roman society?

2. The authors recorded the facts truthfully. a) They were upright, God-fearing men. Time and again in their narratives lying and hypocrisy are scourged in the most unmistakable terms; if they had not told the truth themselves, they would have been more despicable than the hypocrites they condemn. In their teaching and preaching they are the implacable foes of idolatry; how could they, by recounting untrue words of Christ about His Divinity, have deceived the world into deifying a mere man?

> "It suffices to read the Gospels without prejudice to be
> convinced that these historians could not be impostors;
> the honest and candid tone of their narrative is a sure
> warrant of their truthfulness. There is no affectation, no
> bombast, no exaggerated expression in their account, noth-
> ing that denotes passion, or betrays the desire to please."
> (DEVIVIER).

b) Why should the Evangelists have tried to deceive the
world? *Nemo gratis mendax*, no one lies gratuitously; and much
less will anyone lie for the sake of bringing trouble and ruin
upon himself. The Evangelists knew that what they related
was an accusation of the most serious nature against Jews and
Gentiles alike. They had to expect only that which they actually received for their pains: *persecution and even death*. Pascal was right when he said: "I willingly believe historians whose
witnesses are ready to suffer death itself to maintain the truth
of their testimony."

c) And how could the Evangelists have invented their portrait of Christ? How could a few uneducated men have conceived a hero so noble, so pure, so lovable, so tragic, so unlike
any of the great men of Judea, Greece, or Rome? There is only
one explanation for this marvelous portraiture: the Evangelists
copied an original; Jesus Christ must have been such as they
described Him.

> "It is not in this way that men invent," says Rousseau;
> "the story of Socrates, of which no one has any doubt, is
> less strongly attested than the deeds of Jesus Christ. It
> would be more inconceivable that four men should have
> agreed to forge this book, than to believe that one per-
> son had supplied the subject-matter. The Gospel has char-
> acteristics of truth so great, so striking, so inimitable,
> that the inventor of such a work would be a more won-
> derful man than its hero."

d) The narratives of the four Gospels appear at some points
to contradict one another, and it is only by careful investigation
that they can be harmonized. These apparent contradictions
furnish an additional argument in favor of the veracity of
the Evangelists. If Matthew, Mark, and Luke had been impos-
tors they would certainly have avoided even the appearance of
contradiction.

If we wish to know how Gospels with myths and inventions are written, we have only to glance at the *Apocryphal Gospels*. These were written in the second century and are evidently counterfeits. Their very existence proves the existence of true Gospels.

3. The authors had to tell the truth. When they wrote, many of those who had seen and heard Jesus were still alive. Hence they could not have published false accounts of His words and deeds without being detected and taken to task.

4. We need not stop to discuss the multitude of theories on the origin of the Gospels devised by the enemies of Christianity during the last century and a half. Most of them are abandoned today by all serious scholars. Adolf Harnack, a biblical critic of the highest repute among Rationalists and Modernists, says: "The most ancient literature of the Church is, on all chief points and in the majority of details, *veracious and worthy of belief* from the point of view of literary history." In his most recent works he says that the Synoptic Gospels were written before 70 A.D. The Gospel of St. John, which he places between the years 80 and 118 A.D., he describes as an elucidated St. Matthew and adds: "If we have called St. John an elucidated St. Matthew because his aim also is didactic and apologetic, we may with equal justice call him an elucidated St. Mark and St. Luke, for he shares in the aims which dominate both these Evangelists. By means of the historical narrative he strives, like St. Mark, to show that Jesus is the Son of God, and, like St. Luke, to prove that He is the Savior of the world, in opposition to the unbelieving Jews and the disciples of St. John the Baptist."

"We may well regard the conclusions of Harnack as a triumph for the Church. He makes three most important admissions: first, that the dates the Church has always assigned to the Gospels are substantially correct; secondly, that the Gospels are historical; and thirdly, that they represent Christ as claiming to be the Son of God. The New Testament documents have been tried in the furnace of hostile criticism and have emerged unscathed." (SHEEHAN).

3. The Acts of the Apostles

1. From the opening words of the *Acts of the Apostles* and the Gospel of St. Luke it is certain that the same man wrote

Socrates

both books, and that the *Acts* are a continuation of the Gospel. The Lucan authorship of the Acts is confirmed by the "We" sections of that book: 16:10-17; 20:5-15; 21:1-18; 27:1-28.

2. The so-called *Muratorian Fragment* (second century), which contains a list of the Sacred Scriptures, says: "But the *Acts of the Apostles* are written in one book. Luke wrote them for the excellent Theophilus, because he was an eye-witness of the events." *St. Irenaeus,* who quotes several passages from the Acts, says that St. Luke was the companion of St. Paul and the historian of his labors.

3. St. Luke's historical trustworthiness and his accuracy in geographical and political data are admitted by all critics. "St. Luke," writes Rackham in his *Commentary on the Acts,* "is equally at home with the Sanhedrin and its parties, the priests and the temple guard, and the Herodian princes at Jerusalem, with the proconsul of Cyprus and Achaia, the *rulers of the Synagogue* and the *first men* of Antioch in Pisidia, *the priest of Zeus* at Lystra, the *praetors, lictors,* and *jailer* at Philippi, the *politarchs* of Thessalonica, the *Areopagus* of Athens, the *Asiarchs* with the *people, assembly* and *secretary* at Ephesus, the *centurions, tribune* and *procurator* of Judaea, the *first man* of Malta, and the *captain of the camp* at Rome. Such accuracy would have been almost impossible for a writer compiling the history fifty years later. In some cases where his statements had been impugned, St. Luke has been signally vindicated by the discovery of inscriptions, as in the case of the politarch of Thessalonica and the proconsul of Cyprus."

4. The *Acts* were certainly written before A.D. 70, because Jerusalem and the Temple are mentioned as still in existence.

Conclusion. A passage from De Broglie admirably sums up the case of the four Gospels: "Four narratives, simple in form, precise, harmonious and consonant in their account, written by ocular or contemporary witnesses, in a language perfectly intelligible, these are the documents on which is founded the religion of Jesus Christ. The concert of ancient testimonies, the prompt diffusion of its tenets, the resemblance of texts spread over the whole world, the conformity of the narrative with contemporary chronology, these are the titles that give to the Gospel writings such a value as to make them take the first rank with the authentic monuments of the past. We ask for the Gospels no other favor than this, that they be not ostracized or deprived of the common right which is sanctioned by honest criticism and the impartial verdict of mankind." (*The Church and the Roman Empire*).

We may now proceed to look at the New Testament documents and see what picture of Christ and His teaching they present.

SUPPLEMENTARY READING

The Apostles Were Reliable Witnesses

The Apostles were simple, literal-minded men; not superstitious, and still less romantic; free from all traces of morbidness; slow of belief, through a lack of imagination; as individuals strikingly different in character, so as not easily to be led the same way; with the exception of St. John not well adapted to be theologians, and none of them (like St. Paul) controversial theologians; but singularly well qualified as witnesses. They were qualified as witnesses because, free from all preoccupation with ideas and systems, they were plain men who could receive the impress of facts; who can tell a simple plain tale and show by their lives how much they believed it.

—C. GORE, *The Incarnation of the Son of God*, New York: Charles Scribner's Sons, p. 81.

The Apostles Were Not Deceivers

The hypothesis of deceptive Apostles is very absurd. Let one follow it, throughout; let one imagine these twelve men, assembled after the death of Jesus Christ, conspiring together to say that he was raised from the dead: they attack thereby all powers. The heart of man is strangely inclined to levity, to change, to promises, to possessions. However little one of them might have been shaken by these attractions, and, what is more, by prisons, tortures and death, they had been lost. Let one follow this out.

—PASCAL, *Thoughts*, New York: G. P. Putnam's Sons.

The Apostles Did Not Invent the Doctrine They Preached

Who among his disciples or among their proselytes was capable of inventing the sayings ascribed to Jesus or of imagining the life and character revealed in the Gospels? Certainly not the fishermen of Galilee, as certainly not St. Paul, whose character and idiosyncrasies were of a totally different sort; still less the early Christian writers in whom nothing is more evident than that the good which was in them was all derived, as they always professed that it was derived, from the higher source.

—JOHN STUART MILL, *Three Essays on Religion*, New York: Longmans, Green and Co., p. 253.

SUGGESTIONS FOR STUDY AND REVIEW

1. Why do the non-Christian contemporaries of the Apostles tell us so little about Christ and Christianity?
2. What facts does Tacitus record about Christ?
3. What does Pliny tell us about the belief and manner of life of the early Christians?
4. What testimony does Josephus bear to Christ?
5. Which Epistles of St. Paul are regarded as genuine even by Rationalists?
6. What is the central theme of the preaching of St. Paul?
7. By what three tests can the historical authority of a book be established?

8. Explain the terms Gospel, Evangelist, Synoptic Gospels.
9. What is the Synoptic Problem?
10. Write a brief account of the four Evangelists.
11. How can we prove that a work is genuine?
12. Show that the Gospels existed in the earliest days of the Church.
13. What does an examination of the Gospels themselves reveal in regard to their authors?
14. Show from the public character of the Gospels that they could not have been tampered with.
15. Which are the most ancient manuscripts and translations of the Gospels?
16. Show that there is stronger evidence for the integrity of the Gospels than for the integrity of the classics.
17. Show that the Evangelists could know the facts they record.
18. Why could they not have invented the portrait of Christ?
19. Show that the Evangelists had to tell the truth.
20. Why is there no doubt in regard to the historical authority of the Acts of the Apostles?
21. Write a brief paragraph on each of the following: *Tacitus, Pliny the Younger, Suetonius, Josephus (Flavius), Talmud, Harnack (Adolf), St. Clement of Rome, St. Ignatius of Antioch, St. Justin Martyr, St. Irenaeus, Tertullian, Origen, Philo, St. Jerome, Apocryphal Gospels, Tuebingen School, Muratorian Fragment.*

SUGGESTED READINGS

Catholic Encyclopedia, Articles on the New Testament.
Courbet, P., *Jesus Christ is God*, section on the Gospels (C.T.S.).
Chesterton, G. K., *The Everlasting Man*, pp. 220 ff.
Messmer, Most Rev. S. G., *Outline of Bible Knowledge*, sections dealing with the New Testament.

CHAPTER III

The Claims of Jesus

A. Jesus Claimed to Be the Messias

There is no doubt whatever that Jesus claimed to be the Messias (the Christ) whose coming had been foretold by the prophets of the Old Law.

a) Since the time of the Prophet Daniel *Son of Man* is the name of the *Messias,* the anointed envoy of God and the Savior of the world. "I beheld in the vision of the night, and lo, one like the *Son of Man* came with the clouds of heaven, and he came even to the Ancient of Days, and they presented him before him. And he gave him power, and glory, and a kingdom; and all peoples, tribes and tongues shall serve him; his power is an everlasting power that shall not be taken away, and his kingdom shall not be destroyed." (*Dan.* 7:13-14).

No less than eighty times Jesus calls Himself the *Son of Man*, sixty-eight times in the Synoptic Gospels and twelve times in the Gospel of St. John.

b) When Peter made his great profession of faith at Caesarea-Philippi: "Thou art the Christ (the Messias), the Son of the living God," Jesus praised and blessed him and declared that this knowledge had been revealed to him by God.

c) The Messias was expected at the time when Jesus was born. When the Jews asked John the Baptist who he was, he answered: "I am not the Messias." John's own disciples asked Jesus: "Art Thou He that is to come, or look we for another?" The miracle of the multiplication of the loaves called forth from all who witnessed it the exclamation: "This is the prophet indeed that is to come into the world." From Virgil we know that even beyond the limits of Palestine a tradition of the coming Liberator was cherished (*Eclogue IV*). The Emperor Augustus himself wanted to be looked upon as the Savior of the world who put an end to warfare and strife (Inscription of Priene in Asia Minor).

The Jews expected a Messias who would be a great political leader, restore the kingdom of Israel, and conquer all nations.

Jesus corrected this false notion. He claims that His mission is a purely spiritual mission and His kingdom not of this world. He is the teacher of Justice and of the New Law of Love;

75

Perugino

"Jesus saith to them: 'But whom do you say that I am?' Simon Peter
answered and said: 'Thou art Christ the Son of the living God.'
And Jesus answering said to him: 'Blessed art thou,
Simon Bar-Jona: because flesh and blood hath not revealed it
to thee, but My Father Who is in Heaven.'" (*Matt.* 16:13-17)

Collect. Natalis

"Go and relate to John what you have heard and seen. 'The blind
see, the lame walk, the lepers are cleansed, the deaf hear, the dead
rise again,the poor have the gospel preached to them.'" (*Matt.* 11:2-5)

He is the Liberator from the slavery of sin, who not only forgives sin, but also gives His life for the redemption of the many (See the Sermon on the Mount; *Matt.* 9:6; *Mark* 10:45). He will rise again from the dead (*Matt.* 16:21), and come again for the Great Judgment (*Matt.* 25:31).

By this consciousness of a *religious Messiahship* Jesus connects His person and His mission with the great Messianic prophecies of the Old Testament, especially with that of Isaias, which foretold the coming of the Prince of Peace, the King of Justice, the Servant of Jahve who offers himself as a sacrifice and a ransom (*Is.* 53).

B. Jesus Claimed to Be the Son of God

The expression *Son of God* was in ordinary use among the Hebrews to indicate a man of great wisdom and piety. It was not in this sense that Christ made use of it; for then it would not have caused such a sensation. The question that the Jews had raised was this: **Did Jesus make Himself the Son of God by nature, and therefore true God?** From the Gospel record of His words and deeds it is clear that He did.

a) Whenever Christ touches on His relationship with the Father He always says: "*My* Father"; but when He speaks of His disciples He invariably says: "*Your* Father." He never speaks of "*Our* Father." The Lord's Prayer is no exception, because this prayer was composed by Him expressly for His Apostles, as we know from His own words: "Thus shall *ye* pray." The distinction is very precisely drawn in the cases where both expressions occur in one sentence: "Come ye blessed of *My* Father, possess you the kingdom prepared for you from the foundation of the world" (*Matt.* 25:34).

b) When His Blessed Mother said to Him in the Temple: "Son, why hast Thou done so to us? Behold Thy father and I have sought Thee sorrowing," He replied: "Did you not know that I must be about *My Father's* business?" A child of twelve can speak in this way only if he feels himself to be in a very special sense the Son of God.

c) Jesus had sent forth His seventy-two disciples to preach the Gospel, and their mission had met with success. On their return He welcomes them with the joyful words: "I confess to Thee, O Father, Lord of heaven and earth, because Thou hast hidden these things from the wise and prudent, and hast revealed them to little ones. *All things are delivered to Me by*

*My Father, and no one knoweth who the Son is but the Father,
and who the Father is but the Son, and to whom the Son will
reveal Him." (Matt.* 11:25; *Luke* 10:21).

The sense of these words is the same as *John* 1:18: "No man
hath seen God at any time: the only begotten Son, who is in
the bosom of the Father, He hath declared Him." The equality
of the Father and Son as to knowledge is clearly stated, and
this equality implies that both are of the same nature. "The
substance of the Father," says St. Thomas, commenting on this
passage, "is beyond the comprehension of a created intelligence;
so likewise is the substance of the Son, which is known only
by the Father."

d) On the eve of His Passion Christ made a frank avowal of
His Divine Sonship before the Pharisees in the *Parable of the
Wicked Husbandmen (Mark* 12:1-12). The application of the parable is clear. The servants sent by the Master of the Vineyard
are the prophets. His "most dear Son and Heir" was more than
a prophet, more than the anointed of God. The opening words
of the Epistle to the Hebrews are the best commentary on this
parable: "God, who at sundry times spoke by the prophets, in
these days hath spoken to us by *His Son,* whom He hath appointed
heir of all things, by whom also He made the world. Who being
the brightness of His Father's glory, and the figure of His substance sitteth on the right hand of the Majesty on high."

e) When Jesus was arraigned before the Sanhedrin, the High
Priest said to Him: "I adjure Thee by the living God that Thou
tell us if Thou be the Christ, the Son of God." And Jesus saith
to him: "Thou hast said it. Nevertheless, I say to you, Here-
after you shall see the Son of Man sitting on the right hand
of the power of God, and coming in the clouds of heaven. Then
the High Priest rent his garments, saying: He hath blasphemed:
what further need have we of witnesses? Behold now you have
heard the blasphemy." (*Matt.* 26:63-65).

The Sanhedrin, judging that Jesus of Nazareth had profaned
the name of God in arrogating it to Himself, applied to Him
the law against blasphemy, and pronounced sentence of death.
Jesus died rather than renounce His right to the title of Son
of God. He died because He assumed it. On this point there is
no ambiguity, for it is admitted even by the most advanced
Rationalists.

f) Before His Ascension into Heaven Christ said to His Apostles: "All power is given to Me in heaven and on earth. Going,
therefore, teach ye all nations, baptizing them in the name of

the Father, and of the Son, and of the Holy Ghost, teaching them to observe all things whatsoever I have commanded you: and behold I am with you all days, even to the consummation of the world." (*Matt.* 28:18-20).

From this text it is clear that the Son is equal to the Father and the Holy Ghost, that He is omnipotent, and that He promises to be with His followers unto the end of the world, which can be said of God alone.

In conclusion we may ask with Father Knox: "If Jesus did not claim to be God, what did He claim to be? If He was conscious of belonging to any order of being less than divine, how could He have answered the challenge of the High Priest without a word of explanation or of self-defense?"

C. Some Difficulties Solved

1. Rationalists and Modernists maintain that Our Lord's consciousness of His Messiahship and Divine Filiation was a notion which dawned on Him gradually and strengthened as He grew older.

"This is pure speculation," says Father Ronald Knox, "which sins by going beyond the evidence. The evidence is not that the consciousness dawned gradually upon Him, but that He allowed it to dawn gradually on the rest of the world. The fact that He forbade the devils to call Him Christ early in His ministry, yet encouraged Peter to call Him Christ later in His ministry, does not define the limit of what He knew, but what He wished to be known. And there can be little doubt in any candid mind which reads the four records merely as records that His self-revelation was a gradual revelation. It was natural, if not necessary, that it should be. The Jews, it is clear, were not expecting a Messiah who should come amongst them as a man amongst men; they looked for a Deliverer from the clouds. Their ideas, therefore, had to be gradually remodelled. Their minds had to be accustomed gradually to the idea that this was something more than Man." (*The Belief of Catholics*, New York: Harper and Brothers, p. 104).

2. In their hatred of Christ some writers have even gone so far as to maintain that He was the victim of hallucination, or in plain words, a madman and lunatic. In support of their blasphemous contention they point to such incidents as the casting out of the buyers and sellers from the Temple.

But surely, when a person who feels and lives his religion

sees the House of God desecrated and turned into a market-
place and a money-lenders' booth, it is not a symptom of mad-
ness if he makes "as it were a scourge of little cords" and drives
out the profaners of the sanctuary.

**3. Others declare that Our Lord showed signs of abnor-
mality by preaching hatred of the family.**

Christ did say: "Who is My mother, and who are My brethren? Whosoever doth the will of God, he is brother and sister
and mother to Me." (*Mark* 3:33-35). But these words are not a
denial of the claims of family ties, nor do they imply any cen-
sure of His Mother and brethren. Jesus merely asserts that
there are far stronger and higher claims. We do not call those
madmen, but heroes, who set their calling in life, their duty to
their God, their country, and their fellow-men above their duty
towards their families. On the cross Christ showed how much
He loved His Mother. The Gospels are full of incidents which
show what a tender, loving Heart Jesus had. Remember His
tender behavior towards Lazarus and his sisters and the little
children whom their mothers brought to Him, or His tears over
Jerusalem, or His conduct towards Peter, before and after his
denial of Him, or towards Thomas when he doubted, or towards
Judas who betrayed Him.

But did not the friends of Jesus think that He was mad?
"And when His friends heard of it, they went out to lay hold
of Him. For they said: He is become mad." (*Mark* 3:21).

We answer: In the first place, the words: "He is become
mad," are much too strong; "He is beside Himself," would be
the more correct rendering of the original Greek. Secondly, the
words quoted must be read with the foregoing verse in order
to understand why His friends entertained the misguided notion
that Our Lord was beside Himself: "And He cometh to His
home; and again the multitude cometh together, so that they
could not even take food. And when His friends (or His own
people) heard of it, they came out to lay hold of Him, for they
said 'He is beside Himself.' " Evidently his relatives and friends
wished to force Him to take more care of Himself; and Our
Lord does not blame them for their solicitude. St. John (7:5)
tells us that His own relatives did not as yet believe in Him;
that is, they did not believe that He was the Messias. It is not
so strange, therefore, that they should have believed He was
beside Himself, when they saw Him so exclusively occupied
with preaching, healing the sick, and disputing with the Scribes
that He neglected to eat and drink and rest.

4. The very extravagance of His claims, others tell us, is proof enough that Christ was a religious fanatic.

It is true that Jesus believes that before He became Man He dwelt in the glory of the Father; He believes that He is consubstantial with the Father; He believes that He will come again to judge mankind—but we fail to discover even the faintest trace of hallucination or lunacy in His character. The religious maniacs in and out of our insane asylums betray all the symptoms of degeneracy. Their powers of reasoning are woefully warped. Their actions are anything but in harmony with their claims. They are proud and weak-minded, selfish and vindictive, without self-knowledge, full of fantastic dreams for the betterment of the world. Jesus is the direct opposite of all this. Humility and self-sacrificing love, hatred of shams and hypocrisy, keenness of intellect, astounding knowledge of men and of the workings of the human heart, are among the outstanding traits of His Personality.

> "The suggestion of madness is inconsistent with the breadth of vision and the originality of thought (to put it at its lowest) which are displayed by our Lord's teaching. In madness there may be glimpses of inspiration . . . but, on the average, that liberation of the unconscious which is secured by madness, by drug-taking and by certain other influences is lamentably disappointing in its results. The letters of lunatics . . . how inexpressibly *boring* they are, to say nothing of their other qualities! The results obtained by automatic writing, or by spiritualistic mediumship, how signally they have failed to enrich the world's literature by a single new thought! . . . But surely, if every vestige of the Christian religion should disappear from the planet, the words spoken by Jesus of Nazareth would still be read for their own beauty. Agree with them or disagree with them, do they not provide *food for thought* beyond anything which the pale mystics of the East have ever achieved? Are they not, whatever they are, a permanent addition to the triumphs of the human genius?" (KNOX, *The Belief of Catholics*, p. 116).

5. "My God, My God, why hast Thou forsaken Me?" These words of Christ on the cross present a difficulty to many, but they are by no means, as Rationalists would have us believe, a cry of despair. They are taken from the twenty-first Psalm, which is admittedly Messianic. Perhaps Our Lord was passing over in His mind the whole of this Psalm, which foretold so truly the extremity of His human desolation. We must remember that Christ bore the fullness of suffering for us, and since desolation or abandonment—"dark night of the soul" the Mystics call it—is the acutest form of suffering, it was but natural that He should endure that too; that a barrier should have been interposed, as it were, between Himself and the loving countenance of His Father.

6. Speaking of the end of the world, Christ says: "But about that day or that hour no man knoweth, not even the angels in Heaven, nor yet the Son, but only the Father." (*Mark* 13:32). Does not Christ by these words place Himself below God in knowledge?

As Son of God Our Lord knew "that day and hour"; but as the *Son of Man,* as the Messias, He was not commissioned to reveal it to men. When the Apostles asked Him before His Ascension: "Lord, wilt Thou at this time restore again the kingdom to Israel?" He replied: "It is not for you to know the times and moments which the Father hath put in His own power." (*Acts* 1:7). Speaking as Man, Our Lord also said: "The Father is greater than I."

7. In treating of Our Lord's claim to be the Messias and the true Son of God, we have confined ourselves to the *Synoptic Gospels,* because many modern critics outside the Catholic Church regard the fourth Gospel as rather "a work of philosophic reflection" than a record of events. But to any candid reader it must be evident that the claims of Jesus recorded in the Gospel of St. John are not essentially different from those made by Him in the Synoptic Gospels.

> "He who was David's Lord and who saw Satan fall like lightning from heaven could surely say, 'before Abraham was, I am' (*John* 8:58), and could elucidate His claims by calling Himself 'the Beginning, which also speaketh with thee.' (*John* 8:25). He who was Lord of angels and devils, who could walk upon the sea, who promised that He would judge the world and who, finally, claimed to share God's incomprehensible nature can hardly surprise us when He says, 'The Father and I are one thing' (*John* 10:30), and, 'He that seeth Me seeth the Father also' (*John* 12:45). He who said in the garden, 'Think you not I could ask My Father and He would give me more than twelve legions of angels,' could surely say, 'I lay down My life for My sheep: no man taketh it from Me. But I lay it down of Myself and I have power to lay it down and I have power

Feuerstein

"They therefore who were come together, asked Him, saying, 'Lord wilt Thou at this time restore again the Kingdom of Israel?' But He said to them, 'It is not for you to know the times or moments which the Father hath put in His own power' . . . and when He had said these things, while they looked on, He was raised up: and a cloud received Him out of their sight." (*Acts* 1:7-9).

to take it up again.' (*John* 10:15-18). He for whom the
sins of the Magdalen were a debt to Himself which He
had power to remit could surely read the heart of the
Samaritan. He who could say, 'Come unto Me all ye who
labor,' could surely say, 'I am the Way, the Truth and the
Life.' (*John* 16:6). Surely Harnack is right when he says
that the fourth Gospel is only an elucidation of the other
three." (LEO WARD, *The Catholic Church and the Appeal
to Reason*, New York: The Macmillan Company, p. 87).

SUPPLEMENTARY READING

The Famous Dilemma of St. Augustine

If the thing believed [Christ's Resurrection and Ascension] is
incredible, it is also incredible that the incredible should have
been so believed. Here we have three incredible things, which
nevertheless have come about. 1) It is incredible that Christ
should have risen in the flesh, and with that flesh ascended
into Heaven; 2) it is incredible that the world should have
believed a thing so incredible; 3) it is incredible that men, destitute of nobility and rank, numbers and skill, should have been
able so effectively to persuade the world, and even the learned
men in it. Of these three incredibles, our opponents refuse to
believe the first; the second they are forced to believe; and how
that second came about they cannot say unless they believe the
third. . . . If our opponents do not believe that the Apostles
worked miracles to prove the Resurrection and Ascension of
Christ, this one tremendous miracle suffices for us—that the
world believed the message of the Apostles without miracles.
                    —ST. AUGUSTINE, *City of God*, Bk. XXII, ch. 5.

The Divinity of Christ Proved by
His Victory over Paganism

How was it that a Jewish peasant, untaught even in the
simple lore of Syrian literature, should have conceived those
truths which have enlarged the sphere of man's knowledge and
made the one grand revolution in the history of his race? How
could his designs have been developed, with a power that shook

the mightiest kingdoms, overthrew all preceding forms either of faith or philosophy, and have finally cast into a new mould the most distant countries and generations of the earth? How was it that one who spoke no language, save a dialect of the Barbarous East, could triumph over the pride of the Porch and the subtility of the Academy? How came the might of thirty legions to yield to the staff and sling of the son of David? What compelled men to admit the paradox of the fervid African, and allow the very strangeness of this truth to stamp it with the character of being divine: *Crucifixus est Dei Filius; non pudet, quia pudendum est: et mortuus est Dei Filius: prorsus credibile est, quia ineptum est; et sepultus resurrexit: certum est, quia impossibile est*—The Son of God is crucified; we are not ashamed of it, because it is something to be ashamed of: and the Son of God died: this is quite credible, because it is absurd; and after being buried, He arose: this is certain, because it is impossible (Tertullian, *De Carne Christi, V.*).

—R. I. WILBERFORCE, *The Doctrine of the Incarnation in Relation to Mankind and the Church*, ch. 5.

SUGGESTIONS FOR STUDY AND REVIEW

1. What is meant by the word Messias?
2. What did Our Lord mean when He called Himself the Son of Man?
3. Quote Peter's profession of faith. How did Christ approve it?
4. Show that the Messias was expected at the time when Jesus was born.
5. What kind of Messias did the Jews expect? What kind did Jesus claim to be?
6. What two meanings can the title Son of God have?
7. Quote two passages from the Synoptic Gospels which prove beyond a doubt that Jesus claimed to be the Son of God in the strict sense of the word.
8. Why did Our Lord reveal His Messiahship only gradually?
9. Show that Christ could not have been the victim of hallucination.
10. Why did his friends on one occasion suggest that He was

beside Himself?
11. Show that the extravagance of His claims does not stamp Him as a religious fanatic.
12. Explain Our Lord's cry on the Cross: "My God, My God, why hast Thou forsaken Me?"
13. Was Christ really ignorant of the day and hour of the Last Judgment?
14. Show that the claims of Jesus recorded by St. John are essentially the same as those made by Him in the Synoptic Gospels.
15. Annotate: *Virgil, Eclogue, Son of Man, Messias, Rationalist.*

SUGGESTED READINGS

Knox, R. A., *The Belief of Catholics*, pp. 104-113.
Stoddard, J. L., *Rebuilding a Lost Faith*, Ch. VIII.
Ward, L., *The Catholic Church and the Appeal to Reason*, pp. 82ff.
Russell, W. H., *Your Religion*, pp. 24ff.

CHAPTER IV
Jesus Justified His Claims

When treating of the proofs for the existence of God, we saw that the reign of law and order in the universe reveals God to us as the All-Wise Master-Artist; that our conscience reveals Him as the All-Holy Lawgiver, and that the very fact of the existence of spirit and matter, life and motion, reveals Him as the All-Powerful Creator.

Now if Jesus of Nazareth really was what He claimed to be, if He was the Christ, the Son of the Living God, then we should naturally expect Him to justify His claims by a similar manifestation of holiness, wisdom and power; in other words, we should expect Him to have lived a life of perfect holiness and to have given proof of His supernatural wisdom and power by miracles and prophecies.

A glance at the Gospel records of His words and actions will satisfy any candid inquirer that He *did* justify His claims by his threefold proof of His Divinity.

A. The Perfect Holiness of Jesus

1. Christ was free from every sin and imperfection. He said to His enemies: "Which of you shall convince Me of sin?" And none dared to reply. He who had the liveliest perception of sin; who thirsted for the conversion of the whole world; who passed His life in calling men to repentance, this man never betrays the faintest suspicion that He Himself may stand in need of repentance and pardon. He says to His disciples: "You, when you pray, shall say: 'Our Father who art in Heaven . . . forgive us our trespasses.'" He Himself never prays thus. He has a pure and spotless conscience; a conscience of sublime peace and serenity, never clouded by a shadow of regret, or remorse, or fear.

But Our Lord's holiness did not merely consist in exemption from sin; it is characterized also by the perfection of every virtue. The Gospels are full of examples of His charity, humility, gentleness, forbearance, patience, love of His enemies, love of prayer.

87

"Although each virtue exists in Him in its full and absolute perfection, it is not prejudicial to the contrary virtue: it rather calls it forth. So that in Him we never see one virtue alone: there are always two absolutely opposite virtues, one as beautiful as the other, and from them spring the most unexpected contrasts, which blend at last in perfect harmony. Who, for example, was more stern than Christ? Yet who was more tender? Who ever had a greater conviction of His own intrinsic glory? Yet who was humbler? We admire His innocence and purity; yet where shall we find a penitent who was more austere? Who ever knew the misery of man as He did? but who has loved men more? who has despised them less? who has expected more from them?

"Since suffering is the touchstone of moral perfection, it is not spared Him. Every trial is brought to bear on Him, in order to make His virtues more resplendent. He was bound to a column, inhumanly scourged, buffeted, insulted, but He uttered no complaint. When Judas betrayed Him with a kiss, when Peter denied Him, when the executioners spat in His face, He had but one word, one look, one prayer, the word of pardon and of love. After He has given everything to the world, His mind, His heart, His life, receiving in exchange suffering, and the infamy of the cross, He is thrilled with joy. Ah! it is a grand thing to do good in this poor world, and to ask no recompense. We bend the knee before those who, forgetting self, sacrifice themselves, and before those, happier still, who are forgotten by those whom they have most loved. But to be hated by them, to be persecuted by them, to do the greatest possible good, to give one's whole life to men—and the purest and most elevated of all lives, and to have no reward, to reap only ingratitude, to sink beneath the weight of one's benefactions, and so to be happy, never has there been anything greater on earth. Yes! I throw a veil over the divinity of Jesus Christ. I look at Him on His cross, having done good by the impulse of the purest love that ever existed, having realized it at the price of the greatest sufferings, and having been paid by ingratitude, and I say that there is the sublime height of moral beauty and virtue. What was the death of Socrates beside this death? What was Plato's ideal of the just man suffering, compared to this reality? True indeed is the saying of Rousseau: 'If the life and death of Socrates are those of a sage, the life and death of Jesus are those of a God'" (BOUGAUD, *The Divinity of Jesus Christ*, pp. 85ff.).

B. The Superhuman Wisdom of Jesus

1. Jesus never attended any of the schools of learning of His day, yet "He taught as one having power" (*Matt.* 7:29), and His hearers asked in astonishment: "How came this man by this wisdom?" (*Matt.* 13:54), and even His enemies had to confess: "Never did man speak like this man." (*John* 7:46).

2. **The doctrine of Jesus is for all peoples and for all Times.** How sublime is His conception of God! God's holiness, goodness, and mercy have never been set forth so touchingly and convincingly by anyone, sage or prophet, since the dawn of time. He reveals the innermost life of God in the mystery of the Blessed Trinity. He gives to the world the new conception of the Fatherhood of God. He does not abrogate the Old Law, but completes and perfects it. The new kingdom of God which He preaches, is a spiritual kingdom: God is Lord over the hearts of men, and judges not only their deeds, but their very thoughts. He proclaims the inestimable value of the human soul: "What doth it profit a man, if he gain the whole world, but suffer the loss of his soul?" In His incomparable similitudes and parables He throws a flood of light on the relationship between God and man, between man and his fellow-man, and unfolds the hidden life of the soul, the workings of God's grace and man's guilt and punishment. His *Our Father* is the absolutely perfect prayer, His *Eight Beatitudes* the simplest and sublimest program of perfection. His *new commandment* is the all-embracing commandment of love, of which the world before Him had no conception.

3. **The doctrine of Christ renewed the face of the earth.**— Wherever men live up to it, peace and happiness and a foretaste of paradise are the immediate fruit; wherever men depart from it, the foundations of society begin to totter and to fall. There is no substitute for the Gospel of Christ. If all men would regulate their lives, in public and private, according to it, there would be no social question to solve, no social evils to eradicate, no world wars to fear, the Golden Age would dawn upon the world. He who taught these doctrines could justly say of Himself: "I am the Way, the Truth and the Life; I am the Light of the world."

4. **Even those who refuse to admit Christ's claim to Divine Filiation cannot but acknowledge His superhuman wisdom and holiness.**

"Let mental culture go on advancing," says Goethe, "let
the natural sciences go on gaining in depth and breadth,
and the human mind expand as it may, it will never go
beyond the elevation and moral culture of Christianity
as it glistens and shines in the Gospel."

Ernest Renan, a radical freethinker, speaks of Christ
as "that sublime person, who presides perpetually over
the destiny of the world." In another place he says: "Jesus
will never be surpassed. His religion will forever grow
young again. All ages will proclaim that among the sons
of men there has not been born a greater than Jesus.
Jesus is without a peer. His glory remains intact. In Him
was concentrated all that is good and elevated in our
nature. Each of us owes to Jesus all that is best in him.
Jesus remains an inexhaustible principle of moral regeneration for humanity. The Sermon on the Mount will never
be excelled. The foundation of true religion is verily His
work. The morality of the Gospel is the most beautiful
code of perfect life which any moralist has traced."

**5. Jesus manifested His superhuman wisdom not only
by the sublimity of His doctrine, but also by foretelling
future events, which God alone could know.** He foretold His
Passion and Resurrection at least three times, clearly and minutely,
when the events could not be foreseen. He predicted the triple
denial of Peter and his martyrdom, the treason of Judas, the
flight of the Apostles during His Passion, the persecutions they
were to suffer for His Name, the destruction of Jerusalem and
the Temple, the dispersion of the Jews, the conversion of the Gentiles, the expansion and continued existence of His Church.

Christ's prophecies were beyond the power of natural prevision or guess. This is especially true in regard to the prediction of His Resurrection on the third day after His death.
It was only by supernatural means that He could foresee it,
because it was a miraculous event and therefore dependent
entirely on the free will of God.

The prophecies of Christ were made by Him in proof of the
Divinity of His mission: "At present I tell you, before it come
to pass; that *when it shall come to pass, you may believe that
I am He.*" (*John* 13:19). If His mission was not divine, God bore
witness to error, which is impossible.

**6. Modernists assert that Jesus announced the imme-
diate end of the world.** They represent Him as an enthusi-
ast and fanatic, who believed that He would come in the clouds

of heaven immediately after His death as the expected Messias in order to judge the present world and inaugurate a new one. Since He promised the world something that was not realized, His claim to Divinity, they argue, must be abandoned.

The majority even of the Rationalist critics discard such an interpretation of Our Lord's prophecy concerning His Second Coming. It is too palpably opposed to the clear teaching of Christ Himself. The best refutation is the beautiful parables, in which He tells of the wonderful but gradual growth of his kingdom from small beginnings, and the Sermon on the Mount, in which we do not find the faintest allusion to the end of the world as a motive for right conduct.

Moreover, Jesus declared in unmistakable terms that no one knows the day of His Second Coming and the end of this present world, and that He Himself has not been commissioned to make any revelation on this point. (*Mark* 13:32; *Acts* 1:6). The uncertainty of the day of His Advent, whether it be at the death of each individual or at the consummation of all things, is to be an incentive to faithful labor and constant watchfulness: "And what I say to you, I say to all, *watch*." (*Mark* 13:37).

> In the great prophecy of His Second Coming (*Matt.* 24; *Mark* 13; *Luke* 21) it is difficult at times to distinguish what refers to the end of Jerusalem and what to the end of the world. The former is a type of the latter, and hence it would not be right to insist on a clear-cut distinction throughout. We must remember that Our Lord's prediction was made in answer to the twofold question of His disciples; "Tell us when shall those things be? and what shall be the signs of Thy coining, and of the consummation of the world?" (*Matt.* 24:3.) Some of His disciples were to witness the destruction of Jerusalem, and the fulfillment of this part of His prophecy was to be for them and for all men the guarantee of the fulfillment of the second part, the final consummation.

C. The Miracles of Christ

1. Christ performed real miracles. He performed actions which the powers of human nature cannot perform, actions which make an exception to all the laws of Creation. He performed such actions often; He performed them in the full light of day, in the streets, in the public places, in the presence of His friends, before immense crowds, under the scrutinizing gaze of His enemies. His contemporaries never called these miracles in question; His enemies attributed them to the influence of the evil spirits. They are so intimately connected with the other facts of His life, with His preaching, passion and death, that they cannot be eliminated without destroying the whole Gospel narrative.

2. The crown of all the miracles of Jesus is His own Resurrection. As a witness to His Divinity it has a threefold value: it is not only a *miracle,* but also the *fulfillment of a prophecy,* and it was the preaching of the *Gospel of the Resurrection* that converted the world to the Religion of Christ.

3. The Resurrection is the fulfillment of a prophecy. To His disciples Jesus said: "The Son of Man shall be betrayed to the chief priests and scribes, and they shall condemn Him to death, and shall deliver Him to the Gentiles to be mocked, and scourged, and crucified, and *the third day He shall rise again.*" (*Matt.* 20:18-19). When His enemies demanded a proof of His Messianic mission, Jesus answered: "Destroy this temple, and in three days I will raise it up. But He spoke of the temple of His body." (*John* 2:19). After His crucifixion His enemies remembered His words and asked Pilate to guard His sepulcher until the third day, "lest perhaps His disciples come and steal Him away and say to the people: He is risen from the dead." (*Matt.* 27:63-64).

4. The Resurrection of Christ is an historical fact. If the history of Christ ended with His death on the cross, we could call Him the wisest of men on account of the sublimity of His doctrine, and the most virtuous of mortals on account of His perfect holiness; the number of His miracles would proclaim Him the greatest of the Prophets, and His passion and death would crown Him as king of martyrs. Jesus would be all this, and more; but He would not be what He Himself claimed to be—He would not be the Messias foretold by the Prophets, the Founder of the Kingdom of God on earth, the Liberator from sin and death, the Mediator between God and men, the Redeemer of the world, the Son of God. "If Christ be not risen again, then is our preaching vain, and your faith is also vain. Yea, and we are found false witnesses of God, that He hath raised up Christ. If Christ be not risen again, your faith is vain, for you are yet in your sins." (*1 Cor.* 15:14).

But Christ is risen from the dead! This is the joyous testimony of the witnesses of His life on earth and of His death on the cross. They proclaim it with one voice, as one man; they

"And they departing made the sepulchre sure,
sealing the stone and setting guards." (*Matt.* 27:66)

"And behold there was a great earthquake. For an angel of the
Lord descended from heaven and coming, rolled back the stone
and sat upon it. And for fear of him, the guards were
struck with terror and became as dead men." (*Matt.* 28:2-4).

proclaim it in spite of insult and mockery and persecution, of imprisonment and torture. Hunger and nakedness and the threat of the sword and the gibbet cannot silence them. They proclaim it to Jew and Gentile, to the learned and the unlearned, to the Scribes and Pharisees in Jerusalem and the Philosophers in Athens, to the Roman governor and to the king of the Jews: "Christ, who died on the cross, whose side was pierced with a lance, whose body lay cold and bloodless in the tomb, is risen from the dead; what we have seen with our eyes and touched with our hands, we declare; we cannot but speak the things which we have seen and heard; by a man came death into the world, and by a man the resurrection of the dead; in Adam all died, in Christ all shall be made alive. God raised up the crucified Nazarene, of this we all are witnesses. He died according to the Scriptures, and was buried, and He rose again the third day according to the Scriptures. He appeared to Peter, and to James, and to all the Apostles; then He was seen by more than five hundred brethren at once. He ate and drank and conversed with us, and before our eyes He was taken up into Heaven. Stephen saw Him standing at the right hand of God; in the splendor of celestial glory He appeared to Saul."

This is the unwavering testimony of the Apostles to the resurrection and the glorified life of Jesus and to His never-ending influence on the fortunes of mankind. This faith is as strongly rooted in them as the consciousness of their own existence.

If their testimony is not true, what testimony is true? If we doubt the simple, definite, unanimous story of the Evangelists, the blood-sealed testimony of the Apostles, can we believe anything? Must we not despair of ever attaining truth on testimony? If these men *were deceived*, then all the impressions registered by our senses, by sight, touch, and hearing, are illusions. It is an illusion when a thousand sane men and women see the sun shine at midday, when ten thousand hear the roar of the storm wind that uproots the giants of the forest. If these men *deceived*, then we are not sure of our lives in the company of our dearest friends. If the Resurrection of Jesus is not a fact, a reality, then all is delusion and an idle dream.

5. The Gospel of the Resurrection converted the world. The Death and Resurrection of Christ is the central theme of the Gospel preached by the Apostles. The world became Christian by believing in the Resurrection. Without the Resurrection Christianity would have been an event more miraculous than

Symbol of the Resurrection on an Early Christian Sarcophagus

the Resurrection itself. For their faith in the Resurrection the martyrs went to torture and death. When the Romans asked them: "How can you adore as God a man who was crucified as a malefactor?" they replied: "He was crucified indeed, and was dead; but He rose from the tomb, and that proves His Divinity."

> "Only the Resurrection was mighty enough to induce the disciples to believe in the Church and the future of Christianity; as for us, we are certain that Christ rose from the dead, because we see the Church" (St. Augustine).

6. Of the many attempts of Rationalism, Modernism, and Unbelief to discredit the Resurrection of Christ some are puerile, others clumsy, and all entirely unsatisfactory and directly opposed to the evidence.

a) To account for the undoubted fact of the *Empty Tomb* the Romans and Jews claimed that the disciples stole the body while the guards were asleep.

b) The eighteenth century Rationalists substituted the suggestion that Christ had not really died, but only swooned.

c) According to Modernists like Loisy, Christ was never buried; the body was thrown into a ditch with the bodies of the malefactors crucified with Him.

d) Dr. Kirsopp Lake thinks that the Holy Women and the disciples mistook the tomb, stumbling by chance upon an empty one.

e) Harnack and his school distinguish between what they call the *Easter Faith* and the *Easter Message.* By the Easter Faith they mean the belief in the immortality of the individual soul; by the Easter Message, the belief in the actual Resurrection of Christ from the tomb. The fact of *the Empty Tomb,* they say, is all that is really historical about the Easter Message. *Why* the tomb was empty, remained unknown to the Holy Women and the disciples, and will forever remain unknown to us. The appearances of the Risen Christ were only visions. We should be satisfied with the assurance that the *Easter Faith* in personal immortality was lighted at the Empty Tomb of Jesus on the first Easter morning and from there conquered the world.

We need reply only to Harnack. According to him it was a combination of *truth*—the immortality of the soul—and error— the Resurrection of Christ, that was witnessed to and preached by the Apostles. But by teaching the immortality of the soul the Apostles were teaching nothing *new* either to Jew or Gentile; for belief in immortality formed a chief element of the religious systems of the Egyptians, the Persians, and the Chaldeans; it was taught by Socrates and Plato, and was part of the instruction imparted to those initiated into the Eleusinian Mysteries and the other Mystery Religions of Greece. Amongst the Jews the Pharisees not only believed in the immortality of the soul, but even in the resurrection of the body. *New* alone would have been the Apostles' Easter Message of Christ's bodily resurrection—new, indeed, but also *untrue* according to Harnack. But can *untrue* news be *good* news, glad tidings, a *Gospel* of true life and eternal salvation? No, a thousand times no: *only true tidings are glad tidings* (Schell, *Christus,* p. 196).

Surely not the story of the Resurrection is fabulous; this epithet, as Father Knox aptly remarks, must rather be reserved for the theories which scholarship has invented to explain it away.

SUGGESTIONS FOR STUDY AND REVIEW

1. How would we naturally expect Christ to justify His claim to be the Son of God?
2. Show that Christ was the holiest of men.
3. How did Jesus manifest His superhuman wisdom?
4. Indicate some of the fundamental doctrines of Jesus.
5. Show what influence the doctrines of Jesus exercised on the world.
6. Show that Christ was a true prophet.
7. Show that Christ was not mistaken in regard to the time of His Second Coming.
8. Why did Christ join the prophecies regarding the fall of Jerusalem and the end of the world?
9. Give four examples of real miracles performed by Christ.
10. Show that Christ's miracles are historical facts.
11. What threefold value has the Resurrection as a witness to Christ's Divinity?
12. Show that the Resurrection was the fulfillment of a prophecy.
13. Prove that the Resurrection is an historical fact.
14. Mention four attempts to discredit the Resurrection. Give a brief answer to each.
15. Explain and refute Harnack's theory in regard to the Resurrection.
16. If Christ had appeared to his enemies after His Resurrection, do you think they would have believed in Him? (Read Cardinal Newman's Sermon: "Miracles No Remedy for Unbelief" and see *Luke* 16:31.)
17. Annotate: *Goethe, Renan, Socrates, Plato, Eleusinian Mysteries.*

SUGGESTED READINGS

Knox, R. A., *The Belief of Catholics*, Ch. IX.
Joyce, G. H., *The Question of Miracles*, Ch. VI.
Newman, Card., *Parochial and Plain Sermons (Selections)*, pp. 196-203 and 432-441.
Bougaud, E., *The Divinity of Christ.*
Sheen, Fulton J., *The Divine Romance.*

Section III

Reasonableness of Our Belief in the Church

Chapter I

The Founding of the Church

God drew near to us in a supernatural manner in the Person of Christ in order to bring comfort to our hearts by taking on a human form.

"*Post haec in terris visus est et cum hominibus conversatus est*—Afterwards He was seen upon earth and conversed with men." (*Baruch* 3:30).

"*Et Verbum caro factum est et habitavit in nobis*—And the Word was made Flesh and dwelt amongst us." (*John* 1:14).

Is it reasonable to suppose, we ask with a noted theologian, that this familiar intercourse of God with man ceased once the visible presence of Christ was withdrawn from amongst us?

1. If we consult the New Testament documents we find that Christ founded not only a Religion, but also a Church, that is, *a visible organization or society composed of those who profess His Religion.* The officers of this organization were commissioned by the Founder to continue His work, above all to preserve His teaching intact and to spread it throughout the world till the end of time.

The word *Church* is derived from the Greek *kyriakon* sc. *doma*, "the Lord's house." The Greek and Latin word *ecclesia*, from which the French *eglise* and the Italian *chiesa* are derived, and the corresponding Hebrew word *kahal*, mean "assembly." Christ borrowed the word from the Old Testament, where it means the "assembly of the congregation of Israel." Very early the word was used to designate either the officers of the assembly, or the individual groups of believers or the buildings set apart for Christian worship. (Cf. the different meanings of the word *school*.)

2. Christ frequently speaks of His Kingdom. He also

98

calls it the Kingdom of Heaven; i.e., the kingdom which came down from Heaven, and the Kingdom of God. The word has a threefold meaning: a) *Eternal Happiness:* "Then shall the King say to them that shall be on His right hand: Come, ye blessed of My Father, possess you the kingdom prepared for you from the foundation of the world." (*Matt.* 25:34). b) *God's Grace,* for which we must be ready to sacrifice all other things; it is the treasure hidden in a field and the pearl of great price. (*Matt.* 13:44-46). c) *A visible body or society of good and bad members:* "The kingdom of heaven is like to a net cast into the sea, and gathering together all kinds of fishes." It is a field in which both wheat and cockle grow together, a wedding feast at which good and bad guests are found, a vineyard for which God hires laborers of every description, a company of wise and foolish virgins. And this kingdom is to endure till the day of reckoning, till the harvest time, till the nuptials; in a word, till the end of the world. Of this kingdom Christ says: "My kingdom is not of this world"; it is not political like other kingdoms, or like the Messianic kingdom expected by the Jews, but spiritual. (*John* 18:36).

3. Christ speaks of His flock. "Fear not, little flock, for it hath pleased your Father to give you a kingdom." (*Luke* 12:32). "And other sheep I have that are not of this fold; them also I must bring, and they shall hear my voice, and there shall be one fold and one shepherd." (*John* 10:16). After the Good Shepherd has withdrawn His visible presence from His flock, it will be pastured and fed by Peter, to whom He said: "Feed My lambs, feed My sheep." (*John* 21:17).

4. Christ calls His Kingdom a Church. Christ seldom used the word *ecclesia,* Church, which was to become the universal designation of His kingdom on earth. All the more emphatic is His use of the word on the occasion of Peter's profession of faith in His Divinity: "I say to thee, thou art Peter, and on this rock I will build My *Church*." (*Matt.* 16:18). On another occasion, speaking of offenders against brotherly love, He says: "If he will not hear them (sc. his brethren), tell the *Church*; and if he will not hear the Church, let him be to thee as the heathen and publican." (*Matt.* 18:17).

5. Christ was invested with the threefold office of Priest, Prophet, and King. The work of Redemption consisted in the discharge of this threefold office. On the eve of His departure from this world Christ delegated His powers to His Apostles: "All power is given to Me in heaven and on earth: going therefore teach ye all nations, baptizing them in the name

Overbeck.

"Feed My lambs, feed My sheep." (*John* 21:7).

of the Father, and of the Son, and of the Holy Ghost, teaching them to observe all things whatsoever I have commanded you: and behold I am with you all days, even to the consummation of the world." (*Matt.* 28:18-20).

From this commission of Christ it is evident that His followers form an organized society under the leadership and guidance of the Apostles and their successors, with the right to teach and to command on the one side, and the duty to be taught and to obey on the other.

6. In order to enable the Church to exercise her three-fold office for the salvation of mankind, Christ promised the assistance of the Holy Ghost. "But the Paraclete, the Holy Ghost, whom the Father will send in My name, He will teach you all things, and bring all things to your mind, whatsoever I shall have said to you." (*John* 14:26).

On the Feast of Pentecost the Holy Ghost descended upon the Apostles. Through Him they received the fullness of sanctification, the perfection of knowledge of Christ's teaching, supernatural strength from on high, and the miraculous gift of tongues.

Thus equipped they issued from the Upper Room, preached to the people, and formed the first company of three thousand souls. (*Acts* 2). Pentecost Day is therefore justly called the *Birthday of the Church.*

7. Thus it is clear that the Church founded by Christ is a visible Church, not a purely spiritual association.— The Church of Christ is a *public* society consisting of rulers and subjects. This society had to be public and visible in order that those desirous of salvation might be able to find it and join it. Evidently Christ did not intend His Church to be a secret organization, much less a purely interior profession of faith in His doctrines. Everything is visible about His great institution: *Baptism,* which is necessary for membership, the other *Sacraments* which He commanded His followers to receive, the *rulers* and *lawgivers* whom the faithful must obey, the *tribunal* before which the faithful are judged and to which they have a right to appeal.

Supplementary Readings

Digitus Dei Est Hic—The Finger of God Is Here

If twelve men without influence, without knowledge, inexperienced in the ways of the world, but loving Christ profoundly,

"And sitting He taught the multitudes out of the ship." (*Luke* 5:3).

have succeeded by the aid of some poor Jews in spreading the
Christian Faith throughout the Roman Empire; if *they* have
accomplished what Greece with all its eloquence, and Rome with
its military power have failed to achieve; if they have succeeded
in founding an institution which has lasted nineteen centuries—
an institution which has regenerated the world, emancipated
the slave, rehabilitated woman, dignified family life, comforted
the afflicted, uprooted vices, taught sublime truths, pure morality and heroic virtue, an institution which has resisted long-
continued and dangerous destructive tendencies, undergone
centuries of persecution, witnessed the passing away of kingdoms and peoples, remaining itself erect and immovable upon
the ruins of time—an institution which has opposed human
interests and passions—surely we have here the greatest of miracles. Unless the principle of causality be denied or the cogency
of evidence called in question, it is necessary to recognize that
this institution is Divine. *Digitus Dei est hic.*

—FRANÇOIS DE LAMY, *Vérité Evidente
de la Religion Chrétienne.*

Golgotha, the Line of
Demarcation in the World's History

There is a line of demarcation which separates into two
grand divisions the history of mankind. It is the line which
bears on its summit the Cross of Golgotha. And why? Because
it is there that was heard the *Fiat Lux* of a second creation;
because thence there came down upon the world the new law
of a new civilization, the New Commandment, as Christ Himself called it. On the day when it was said to the individual:
"Love God above all things and thy neighbor as thyself for the
love of God"; to the citizen: "Render to God the things that are
God's and to Caesar the things that are Caesar's"; and to the
State: "Seek first the kingdom of God and His justice"—on that
day there arose a new morality, a new public law, a new social
ideal. Like mysterious leaven, the creative word worked upon
and permeated humanity, and all the manifestations of justice
and love there produced from century to century are but the
result of this marvelous fermentation: "The kingdom of Heaven
is like to a leaven which a woman took and hid in three mea-
sures of meal until the whole was leavened."

On the day when the Christian religion gave to mankind its
compass and pointed out its polar star, there began for human-

ity a life worth living, a life of which the ancient poet seemed to have had an obscure presentiment when on the frontispiece of the new world he wrote this grand verse:

> *Magnus ab integro saeculorum nescitur ordo.*
> The great order of ages is born anew (Virgil).

Then, walking under the shadow of the Cross, the Christian centuries took the road of the future.

> *Vexilla Regis prodeunt.*
> *Crucis fulget mysterium.*
> The royal banners are unfurled.
> The mystic Cross illumines the world.

> —GODREY KURTH, *What Are the Middle Ages*
> (tr. by V. DAY), pp. 33-34.

Christus Vivit . . .

Christ is not yet expelled from the earth either by the ravages of time or by the efforts of men. His memory is everywhere: on the walls of the churches and the schools, on the tops of bell towers and of mountains, at the heads of beds and over tombs, thousands of crosses bring to mind the death of the Crucified One. Take away the frescoes from the churches, carry off the pictures from the altars and from the houses, and the life of Christ fills museums and picture galleries. Throw away breviaries and missals, and you find His name and His words in all the books of literature. Even oaths are an involuntary remembrance of His presence.

When all is said and done, Christ is an end and a beginning, an abyss of divine mystery between two divisions of human history. Paganism and Christianity can never be welded together. Before Christ and After Christ! Our era, our civilization, our life, begins with the birth of Christ. We can seek out what comes before Christ, we can acquire information about it, but it is no longer ours, it is signed with other signs, limited by other systems, no longer moves our passions; it may be beautiful, but it is dead. Caesar was more talked about in his time than Jesus, and Plato taught more science than Christ. People still discuss the Roman ruler and the Greek philosopher, but who nowadays is hotly for Caesar or against him; and where now are the Platonists and the anti-Platonists?

Christ, on the contrary, is still living among us. There are

still people who love Him and who hate Him. There is a passion for the love of Christ and a passion for His destruction.
The fury of so many against Him is a proof that He is not
dead. The very people who devote themselves to denying His
ideas and His existence pass their lives in bringing His name
to memory.

—GIOVANNI PAPINI, Life of Christ, New York:
Harcourt, Brace and Co., p. 5f.

SUGGESTIONS FOR STUDY AND REVIEW

1. Did Christ break off all intercourse with mankind after
   His Ascension?
2. What various meanings attach to the word *Church?*
3. What terms does Christ use in speaking of the society He
   intended to found?
4. What is meant by the phrase *Kingdom of Heaven?*
5. What is the nature of this kingdom?
6. Quote two texts showing that Christ spoke of His followers as a *flock.*
7. On what two occasions did Christ call His kingdom a
   Church?
8. With what threefold office was Christ invested for the work
   of Redemption?
9. Show that Christ conferred this threefold office on His
   Apostles. What follows from this delegation?
10. Show that Christ promised the assistance of the Holy Ghost
    to His Church.
11. Why is Pentecost called the *Birthday of the Church?*
12. Show that Christ founded a public, visible society.

CHAPTER II

The Constitution of the Church

1. The primitive Church was not a democracy. At its head we find the Apostles, who did not receive their powers from the congregation, but directly from Christ Himself. To them alone, and not to the whole body of His followers, Christ had said: "Teach them to observe all things whatsoever I have commanded you"; to them alone He had said: "He that heareth you, heareth Me, and he that despiseth you, despiseth Me . . . I dispose to you, as My Father hath disposed to Me, a kingdom, that you may eat and drink at My table in My kingdom, and may sit upon thrones judging the twelve tribes of Israel." (*Luke* 10:16; 22:30). The Gospel of St. John bears the same testimony: "As the Father hath sent Me, I also send you . . . You have not chosen Me, but I have chosen you." (*John* 20:21; 15:16). The Apostles themselves were ever conscious of the fact that their authority was from Christ, and they acted accordingly: they never acknowledged any authority higher than their own. "Take heed to yourselves, and to the whole flock, wherein the Holy Ghost hath placed you bishops (overseers), to rule the Church of God, which He hath purchased with His own blood." (*Acts* 20:28).

2. It was the intention of Christ that the authority which He gave to His Apostles should be handed on by them to their successors. He promised His Apostles that He would be with them till the end of the world. (*Matt.* 28:20); they were to live on in their successors as the rulers of the Church. In no other sense could Christ be with them till the end of the world.

The Apostles did, as a matter of fact, bestow their spiritual authority on others. Their first official act after the Ascension of their Master was to provide, in the person of Matthias, a successor to the traitor Judas. They were convinced that "another should obtain his bishopric (overseership), ministry, and apostleship." Later on, by the "laying on of hands and prayer" they consecrated bishops to take their places in the various Christian communities.

St. Clement of Rome, the third successor of St. Peter, writes in the year 96 A.D.: "The Apostles were warned by the Lord that after their death contentions would arise concerning the episcopacy; for this reason they appointed their own successors, and commanded them to see to it that other approved men take up their work after their departure."

4. In the primitive Church the bishops were assisted in their work by priests and deacons. The priests were the representatives of the bishops in the work of the ministry, but they could not bestow their powers on others; i.e., they could not administer the sacrament of Holy Orders. The deacons cared for the poor, the widows, and the orphans, assisted the bishops and priests at the divine service, and occasionally also preached the word of God and baptized.

Originally the distinction between bishops and priests was not clearly drawn, because the Apostles themselves were the spiritual rulers of all the Christian communities. After the death of the Apostles it became necessary to distinguish the names as well as the offices, and the superior were known as bishops, the inferior as priests. But even during the lifetime of St. Paul we find Titus and Timothy enjoying all the powers and exercising all the rights of bishops.

5. Thus from the very beginning the Church presents the picture of Shepherd and Flock, of those who teach and rule and those who are taught and ruled. Speaking of the Church, St. Clement of Rome uses the figure of military discipline: "All the members are by no means generals, captains, and centurions; on the contrary, everyone must remain in his place and do what he is told." According to St. Ignatius of Antioch, the disciple of St. John, Christianity does not simply establish a relation to God and Christ, but also to the bishop, the priest, and the deacon. "Where the bishop is," he writes to the Trallians, "there is the Church." And in another letter he says: "Separated from bishops, priests, and deacons there is no Church."

The Eastern and the Anglican Churches agree with the Catholic Church that Christ instituted a *hierarchy* or sacred authority composed of bishops, priests, and deacons. Protestantism, by doing away with the hierarchy, severed itself entirely from the *Apostolic Church.*

For several centuries the Christian people had a large share in the election of the bishops. No one could become a bishop if the people did not approve of him. But the choice or selection was only a preparatory step. The candidate became a bishop only by consecration through another bishop.

The Election of the Seven Deacons
(*Acts* 6:1-6)

Ordination of the Seven Deacons
"And they praying imposed hands upon them." (*Acts* 6:6)

SUPPLEMENTARY READING

The Church Not a Democracy

"Let us all obey the Bishop, as Jesus Christ obeyed His Father. Let none do apart from the Bishop any of those things which concern the Church. That is to be regarded as a valid Eucharist which is celebrated under the Bishop, or some one whom he has appointed. When the Bishop is present, let the populace be there too, just as where Christ is there is the Catholic Church. It is not lawful to baptize or celebrate the Agape without the Bishop, but whatsoever he shall approve, that same is well-pleasing to God, so that all that is done may be sound and valid . . . It is fitting for men and women who marry, to form this union with the approval of the Bishop, that their union may be according to God."

> —ST. IGNATIUS OF ANTIOCH, *Ep. ad Smyrnaeos*, 8;
> *Ad Polycarpum*, 5.

The Bishops Successors of the Apostles

"In every Church there is opportunity for all those who wish to see the truth to learn the Apostolic tradition made known throughout the world; we can enumerate those who were appointed by the Apostles as Bishops, as also their successors down to our times."

> —ST. IRENAEUS, *Adversus Haereses*, III, I.

SUGGESTIONS FOR STUDY AND REVIEW

1. Show that the primitive Church was not a *Democracy*.
2. Prove that Christ intended that the authority vested in the Apostles should pass on to their successors.
3. Show that the Apostles did hand on their authority to others.
4. What do the words bishop, priest, and deacon mean?
5. Why was there no clear distinction made in the Apostolic Church between bishops and priests?

6. What does the word hierarchy mean? What do St. Clement of Rome and St. Ignatius of Antioch teach concerning the Church and the hierarchy?
7. How were the bishops elected in the Primitive Church? Did election make them bishops?
8. What Churches agree with the Catholic Church in regard to the hierarchy? Why cannot Protestantism lay claim to being the true Church of Christ?
9. What is meant by the *Eastern Church*? The *Anglican Church*?
10. How are bishops chosen in the United States?

CHAPTER III

The Primacy of St. Peter

1. As an Apostolic Church, built upon the foundation of the Twelve Apostles, Jesus Christ being Himself the chief corner stone, the Church of Christ first appears in history. (*Eph.* 2:20). The mark of apostolicity, of historical and real connection with the Twelve, belongs so essentially to it that it cannot be conceived without it. Even the number twelve was of fundamental importance. The Twelve represented the new Israel which was to supersede the old Israel that had rejected the Son of Man. They were conscious of the real significance of their number, and immediately after the Ascension of Jesus it was their first care to fill up the vacancy left in their company by the suicide of Judas.

2. On the occasion of this election one of the Twelve takes a leading part. It is *Simon,* the son of Jonas, surnamed *Peter.* It is he who suggests and conducts the election of Matthias. On the day of Pentecost it is again Simon Peter who speaks in the name of all the Apostles to the assembled multitude. He is also their spokesman before the High Priest and the Sanhedrin. He works astounding miracles. By baptizing the pagan centurion Cornelius he decides the all-important question whether pagans should be received into the Christian Church without circumcision. At the Council of Jerusalem he speaks first—the position of honor in all ancient assemblies—and calms the doubts of his more Judaizing colleague St. James.

Not only in Jerusalem, but also in the vast mission field where St. Paul exercised his apostolate with such astonishing success, the authority of St. Peter is paramount. St. Paul says that with James and John he was one of the "pillars of the Church." St Paul's first visit to Jerusalem after his conversion was made for the purpose "of becoming personally acquainted with Peter." He remained with him fifteen days. (*Gal.* 1:18). He evidently felt the need of assuring himself that he was of one mind with Peter in his teaching.

From the Acts of the Apostles and the Epistles of St. Paul it is clear beyond the possibility of denial that the guidance of the primitive Church devolved upon the Apostles, and that Peter was the head, the "prince" of the Apostles.

3. What is the explanation of this unique position of Peter? He was not the first of the Apostles in the order of time; Andrew and John had followed Jesus before Him. He possessed no greater learning or sanctity than the other Apostles. He was not personally related to Our Lord as some of the others were.

St. Matthew records an event which gives a satisfactory answer to our question. It was in the neighborhood of Caesarea-Philippi at the foot of Mount Hermon, in full view of the mighty cliffs from which the waters of the Jordan issue, that Jesus asked His disciples: "Whom do men say that the Son of Man is? But they said: Some John the Baptist, and other some Elias, and others Jeremias, or one of the prophets. Jesus saith to them: But whom do you say that I am? Simon Peter answered and said: *Thou art Christ, the Son of the living God.*

"And Jesus answering, said to him: Blessed art thou, Simon Bar-Jona: because flesh and blood hath not revealed it to thee, but My Father who is in heaven. And I say to thee: *Thou art Peter; and upon this rock I will build My Church, and the gates of hell shall not prevail against it. And I will give to thee the keys of the kingdom of heaven. And whatsoever thou shalt bind upon earth, it shall be bound also in heaven: and whatsoever thou shalt loose upon earth, it shall be loosed also in heaven.*" (*Matt.* 16:13-20).

Under a triple metaphor the primacy over the Church is promised to Peter: a) He is the rock foundation that guarantees permanence to the Christian body; b) he is the master of the Household of God; the keys symbolize the plenitude of his power over souls; c) he receives the power to impose obligations on the members of the Church and to relieve them of them, and the exercise of this power is ratified in advance by God. The power of "binding and loosing" was afterwards conferred on all the Apostles collectively. (*John* 20:22-23); but to none of them except Peter did Christ say that he was the rock on which His Church was built, and the power of the keys was given to Peter individually and in a special manner.

If we look at the diction of the great promise of Christ, says Dr. Carl Adam, it is immediately evident that the words were originally spoken in Aramaic. The play on the word *Kephas* is possible only in Aramaic. The expressions Simon Bar-Jona, Gates of Hell, Keys of the Kingdom of Heaven, Binding and Loosing, the contrast between Heaven and Earth, are all purely Semitic imagery. There can be no question of a Greek or Roman falsification. But are the verses *genuine?* Do they belong to the original Gospel of Matthew? Or are they a later interpolation? The Protestant theologian Bolliger answers: "The verses fit the context in which they stand as perfectly as a limb fits the body to which it belongs. They bear about them the inimitable perfume of an historically great moment. In form, too, they are such as the great ones of earth, and they only in the greatest hours of their life, can achieve. An interpolator is simply incapable of such an effect."

4. The words of Christ concerning Peter (the Rock-man) were well known both to the Jewish Christians of Palestine and to the converts from paganism long before St. Matthew wrote his Gospel. For both Mark (3:16) and John (1:42) relate that Peter's original name was Simon and that Jesus Himself gave him the name Kephas (Peter, Rock). This name became his proper name. St. Paul calls him Kephas and Peter, while the *Acts of the Apostles* always speaks of him as Peter. Under this name he was known in Jerusalem and Antioch, in Galatia, in Corinth, and in Rome. This fact is all the more remarkable because at the time of Christ neither Kephas nor Peter was a proper name.

5. After the Last Supper Christ again promised the

Raphael

"And Jesus saith to Simon: 'Fear not:
from henceforth thou shalt catch men.'" (*Luke* 5:10).

primacy to Peter. "And the Lord said: Simon, Simon, behold Satan hath desired to have you that he may sift you as wheat. But *I have prayed for thee that thy faith fail not, and thou being once converted confirm thy brethren.*" (*Luke* 22:31-32). Christ's prayer—the prayer of God—was necessarily effective; by it Peter was permanently confirmed in the faith which never failed him, though his moral courage did. Christ prayed for all His Apostles (*John* 17:9ff.); but he prayed in an especial manner for Peter, upon whom the duty devolved of "strengthening his brethren." It is the only record we have of Our Lord offering prayer for an individual. This fact alone helps us to define Peter's relation to his fellow-Apostles.

6. **The primacy which Christ had promised so solemnly to Peter at Caesarea-Philippi was just as solemnly conferred on him after the Resurrection at the Sea of Galilee.** Three times the risen Lord asked Peter: "Lovest thou Me?" And after Peter's threefold assurance: "Lord, Thou knowest that I love Thee," the Good Shepherd makes Peter shepherd in succession to Himself. "Feed My lambs, feed My sheep." (*John* 21:15-17).

There can be no doubt as to the meaning of Christ's words. In the language of the Old Testament (cf. *Ezech.* 37:22-25) as well as in the Greek language kings and rulers are called shepherds of the people. To Peter is given the office of leader and ruler of Christ's people. He is not *primus inter pares*—"the first among his peers," as the Anglicans and Episcopalians would have us believe, but he is their Shepherd, their guide and leader, their Supreme Head.

SUPPLEMENTARY READING

St. Peter Labored and Died in Rome: The Testimony of Archeology

"For the archeologist the presence of Sts. Peter and Paul in Rome are facts established beyond the shadow of doubt by purely monumental evidence. There was a time when persons belonging to different creeds made it almost a case of conscience to affirm or deny *a priori* these facts according to their

Rubens

The Crucifixion of St. Peter at Rome

acceptance or rejection of the tradition of any particular church. This state of feeling is a matter of the past, at least for those who have followed the progress of recent discoveries and of critical literature."

—RODOLFO LANCIANI, *Pagan and Christian Rome*, p. 123.

St. Ephraem on the Primacy of St. Peter

"Simon, My disciple, I placed thee as the foundation of Holy Church. I had already called thee a 'rock,' for thou art to bear up the entire edifice; thou art to be the inspector of all those who shall build up My Church on earth; if they try to build into it spurious material, it will be for you, the foundation, to repress them; thou art the source and the fountain from which My teaching is drawn; thou art the head of My disciples; through thee will I give drink to all the nations; thine is that life-giving sweetness which I will dispense; thee have I chosen that by My appointment thou mayest be as it were the firstborn and mayest be made heir to My treasure; to thee have I given the keys of My Kingdom. Behold I have made thee ruler over all My treasures."

—ST. EPHRAEM THE SYRIAN (306-373),
In Hebdomadam Sanctam, IV, I.

SUGGESTIONS FOR STUDY AND REVIEW

1. Why did Christ choose twelve Apostles, no more and no less?
2. Give facts showing that Peter acted as head of the Apostles.
3. When and in what terms did Christ promise the *primacy* to Peter?
4. Show that the passage *Matt.* 16:13-20 is *genuine*.
5. From *John* 21:15-17 show that Christ fulfilled His promise to Peter.
6. What do Anglicans and Episcopalians hold in regard to the primacy of Peter?

CHAPTER IV

The Primacy of the Roman Pontiff

1. The Primacy a Permanent Institution. Modern Protestant writers generally admit that St. Peter held a unique position amongst the Apostles, that he enjoyed a certain preeminence of honor; some even concede that a real *primacy of jurisdiction,* a real ruling power over all the faithful, had been conferred on him by Christ; but all agree that whatever powers he possessed were strictly *personal,* and therefore not to be continued in his successors.

The Protestant contention is manifestly wrong; for it is clear from the words with which Our Lord conferred the Primacy on Peter that it was not a personal privilege, such as the power of working miracles or the gift of tongues, but a *permanent institution, necessary for the very existence of the Church.*

The Church which Christ founded is to endure till the end of time, and Peter, according to the promise of Christ, is to be the rock foundation of that Church, giving it unity and strength, and securing it against the gates of hell. But the foundation must last as long as the edifice lasts which is built upon it. Hence the power and authority that made Peter the Rock of the Church must remain intact for all time; his Primacy must be perpetuated in the only possible way, that is, by transmission through a continuous line of successors. Father Joseph Rickaby states the argument as follows:

"Who is Simon Peter after all? A mere man, 'fleeting as a shadow.' He shall perish, but Christ remaineth. (*Heb.* 1:11). How can a dead man, however glorious his sepulcher, who has lain there full eighteen hundred years, be the foundation of a Church that is in the world century after century, and shall be till the end of time? The Church on earth is composed of living men. The foundation must be of the same character as the building: it must be a living foundation. So the state and realm of England pivots, not on King Alfred, but upon King George. Thus it is, that Simon perishes, but Peter (like Christ) remains. Peter lives on in his successors." (*Thought,* New York: America Press, 1927).

2. But, it will be asked, who are the successors of St. Peter to whom his powers. and prerogatives passed on?

116

History answers: The *Bishops of Rome.* "Every vestige of Christian tradition traces back the pedigree of the Roman Bishops to Peter." St. Peter lived and labored and died a martyr's death in Rome. The Bishops of Rome have always claimed to be the successors of St. Peter, the heirs of his Primacy. No other See in Christendom ever made such a claim. St. Peter ruled the Church of Antioch before he went to Rome, yet Antioch never disputed the right of Rome to the unique dignity of Apostolic Primacy. Ephesus and Smyrna and the other Churches of Asia Minor over which St. John, the Beloved Disciple, presided long after Peter's death never contested the claim of Rome.

The earliest witness to the residence of Peter in Rome is the *First Epistle of St. Peter,* for it is practically certain that the reference to Babylon must be interpreted as meaning Rome. St. Clement of Rome (A.D. 96) refers to Peter and Paul as martyrs and says that "to these men . . . there was gathered a great company of the elect who became an example to us" (1 Clement 5-6). St. Ignatius, Martyr, writes to the Romans: "I do not command you as Peter and Paul." The suggestion obviously is that the Romans had been instructed by these Apostles. By the end of the second century the tradition is met with everywhere *(Encyclopaedia Britannica,* Art. St. Peter). "St. Peter's work and martyrdom in Rome," writes Blenkin, an English Biblical scholar, "are attested by evidence so early, so wide-spread and so unanimous that even the most determined opponent of Papal claims could not dispute it with any success" (*Cambridge Greek Testament for Schools and Colleges,* p. xvi).

3. The Bishops of Rome were at all times conscious of their supreme ruling power and exercised it whenever occasion arose. There never was a Rome-free Church. Union with the Roman See was always regarded as a fundamental requisite of Unity, Apostolicity, and Catholicity. "With this Church of Rome," writes St. Irenaeus at the end of the second century, "on account of her superior headship, it is necessary that every other church should be in communion."

The first exercise of the Primacy of which a record has come down to us, occurred in the year 96 A.D. "In the time of Clement," writes St. Irenaeus, "no small dissension having occurred at Corinth, the Church in Rome dispatched a most powerful letter to the Corinthians, bringing them to peace, renewing their faith, and declaring the tradition which it had lately received from the Apostles." This letter is still extant, and all critics admit that it was written by St. Clement of Rome, the third successor of St. Peter, who, as the same Irenaeus says, "having seen the Apostles, and having been conversant with them, might be said to have the preaching of the Apostles still ringing in his ears, and their traditions before his eyes."

It is not certain whether the Corinthians had appealed to Rome or whether the Pope intervened of his own accord (*motu*

The Pope's Altar and the Tomb of St. Peter in St. Peter's, Rome

proprio), but it is certain that Clement acted with *full power.* This fact is all the more remarkable as the Apostle St. John was still alive at the time and presiding over the Church of Ephesus. One passage of Clement's letter will suffice to show the tone of authority which he used: "But if any will not obey these things which *Christ has spoken through us*, let them know that they will be implicating themselves in no small danger and offence." Clement evidently claims Divine authority. Yet in spite of this imperious tone and the claim of Divine authority, there was not the slightest protest on the part of the Corinthians. For many years the letter was read at Corinth during divine services and even numbered among the inspired works of Scripture, as Eusebius informs us. The Corinthians must have accepted this "first step toward papal domination," as an Anglican bishop calls it, as in full accord with the teaching of Christ and His Apostles (Berry, *The Church of Christ*, p. 373).

4. **The exercise of the Primacy by the Popes gradually increased with the growth of the Church.** Many powers latent in the Primacy were not fully realized, much less exercised, by the successors of St. Peter until the welfare of the Church demanded it. This is true of all governmental powers—as a glance, for example, at the history of the United States Government proves—and was therefore to be expected in the Church.

5. **The Primacy does not confer a higher power of Order.** There is no higher Holy Order in the Church than the Episcopacy. The Pope takes rank in the Hierarchy of the Church, not as Pope, but as Bishop of Rome. The Primacy confers the *power to rule the whole Church of God.* The limits of this power, are fixed by the spiritual purpose of the Church; hence the Primacy cannot confer any temporal power. If the Popes in the Middle Ages deposed temporal rulers, it was not because the Primacy gave them the right and the power to do so, but by virtue of international law or custom, recognized by all as conferring such authority upon them. Another limit set to the powers of the Pope are the divinely guaranteed rights of the Bishops of the Church to rule their dioceses. (*Acts* 20:28).

6. **The Pope does not receive his power to rule the Church from the Bishops or from those who elect him, but directly from Christ.** The words by which Christ conferred the Primacy on Peter are the *Magna Charta* of the Papacy. They are written in golden letters in the great cupola of St. Peter's Church in Rome: *"Tu es Petrus, et super hanc petram aedificabo*

Raphael

Pope Leo I, the Great, Saves Rome from the Hordes of Attila

ecclesiam meam—Thou art Peter, and on this rock I will build My Church."

7. The *history of the Papacy* during the nineteen centuries of its existence is a proof of its Divine origin. The Papacy has been the source of inestimable blessings for the Church and the world:

a) It has never tired in its efforts to spread the Religion of Christ throughout the world.

b) It saved Christianity from the devastating flood of Islamism.

c) It saved the true faith from the onslaughts of Heresy.

d) It has ever been the bulwark of liberty against Absolutism. It defended liberty of conscience against the pagan emperors of Rome, and the liberty of the Church against the encroachments of the temporal power during the Middle Ages, and the attempts of modern States to bend her to their will.

e) It has ever fought and is still fighting heroically for the protection of the Christian family and its rock foundation, the Sacrament of Matrimony.

8. The opponents of the Papacy often refer to the fact that there were some bad Popes, and that consequently the Papacy itself cannot be a Divine institution.

We concede the fact, but deny the conclusion drawn from it. There were very bad men among the high priests of the

Old Law, and yet the office of high priest was a Divine institution. The successors of St. Peter are frail human beings, just as St. Peter himself, and the Primacy does not confer the prerogative of sinlessness. If among the more than 260 Popes who have ruled the Church up to our time there were some whose lives were scandalous, God no doubt permitted this in order to show that He Himself rules the Church through the Popes; for not one of these so-called "bad Popes" taught a single false doctrine or promulgated an ecclesiastical law that is morally reprehensible.

SUGGESTIONS FOR STUDY AND REVIEW

1. Show that the Primacy conferred by Christ on St. Peter was a permanent institution necessary for the very existence of the Church.
2. Prove that the Bishops of Rome are the successors of St. Peter.
3. What evidence have we for the residence of St. Peter in Rome?
4. Who was St. Clement? On what occasion did he exercise his supreme authority over the Church?
5. What is meant by the expression *motu proprio?*
6. Are there any limits to the ruling power of the Pope?
7. From whom does the Pope receive his power to rule the Church?
8. What do the Church and the world owe to the Papacy?
9. Show that the fact of some Popes having been bad is no argument against the Divine origin of the Primacy.

CHAPTER V

The Infallibility of the Church and the Pope

A. The Church of Christ Must Be Infallible

1. Christianity was preached to the world not as a system of philosophy or human wisdom, but as the Revelation of God. This revelation was communicated to men by Christ, and by the Apostles, who had been instructed by Christ and enlightened by the Holy Ghost. The acceptance of Christianity was, and is, the result of an act of faith in God's revelation.

> "We preach Christ crucified, unto the Jews indeed a stumbling-block and unto the Gentiles foolishness, but unto them that are called, both Jews and Greeks, Christ the power of God and the *wisdom of God.*" (*1 Cor.* 1:23-24).
> "For Christ we are ambassadors, God as it were exhorting through us." (*2 Cor.* 5:20).

2. Infallibility Promised. In order that the glad tidings of salvation might be *faithfully preserved and fully and rightly preached* to the whole world, Christ promised His own assistance and the assistance of the Holy Ghost to His Church, who thus became the "pillar and ground of truth." (*1 Tim.* 3:15).

> "Behold I am with you all days, even to the consummation of the world." (*Matt.* 28:20).
> "I will ask the Father, and He shall give you another Paraclete, that He may abide with you forever, the Spirit of truth. . . . But when He, the Spirit of truth is come, He will teach you all truth." (*John* 14:16; 16:13).

Through the infallible teaching authority of the Church each one of us enjoys the same privilege which the Apostles enjoyed: God's revelation is proposed to us, not by men, but by God Himself.

> "The Church has a human side, of course, as we who are Catholics know all too well. But let us always keep

firm hold on the fact of the divine side of the Church. This is much more important, for it is literally the one solid upstanding rock in a world that seems falling to pieces into chaos. The Church's divine side: it is the life of Christ going on still. The body of men we call the

Pope Pius IX, in whose reign the dogmas of the Infallibility of the Pope and of the Immaculate Conception were declared

Church is Christ's Body, and the mind of the Church is the Mind of Christ (because of the indwelling of the Holy Spirit). She thinks Christ's thoughts and teaches His doctrine, even draws it out further according to need, with the sureness that comes of being identical with Him. 'The things that are to come He shall show you.' She knows her own mind, and knows that it represents His. Remembering His promises, with the Spirit of Truth within her to bring back to her mind whatsoever He has said, she is always sure that she can decide right. So Catholics listen to her voice as to the voice of Christ Himself." (REV. F. H. DRINKWATER).

3. Both reason and history teach us that an infallible teaching authority is necessary in religious matters. Reason tells us that the vast majority of men, from want of time, application, or talent, cannot attain to certain knowledge even of the truths of natural religion. History tells us that wherever the right of individual private judgment was set up as the sole judge in matters pertaining to revelation it has invariably led to disintegration of the Christian faith itself. Protestantism rebelled against the infallible teaching authority of the Church four centuries ago, and how much of the Christianity taught by Christ is there to be found today in the numberless sects into which the rebels divided?

4. The teaching body to which Christ promised infallibility is composed of the Supreme Head of the Church, the Pope, and the Bishops united with him, for they are the successors of St. Peter and the other Apostles, who made up the original teaching body of the Church. Hence when differences arise in matters of faith or morals, the decisions are given either by the Pope or by a Council of Bishops confirmed by the Pope.

B. The Infallibility of the Pope

1. The Infallibility of the Pope, rightly understood, presents no difficulty to anyone who believes that Christ left to His Church an infallible teaching body; for it was this infallible teaching body that solemnly declared at the Vatican Council (1870) that the Pope is protected by a special divine guidance against error whenever he decides upon matters of faith or morals and commands the whole Church to accept his decision.

The Council did not declare that the Pope *cannot sin*; neither did it declare that he can in *no way err*; nor that he cannot *personally* hold erroneous views in matters of faith; but merely that he is infallible, not subject to error, when he decides *ex cathedra*—that is, as Head and Teacher of the whole Church—upon matters of faith and morals.

2. Infallibility does not depend upon the virtue or the learning of the Pope, but on the special assistance of the Holy Ghost, given him according to the promise of Christ, who said to Peter: "I have prayed for thee that thy faith fail not; and thou, being once converted, confirm thy brethren." (*Luke* 22:32).

Hence, in defining the Infallibility of the Successor of St. Peter, the Vatican Council did not introduce a new doctrine, but simply *defined*—i.e., solemnly declared in precise words— the ordinary and normal mode in which Christ willed and provided that His Church should be kept infallibly in the path of Divine truth and saved from the assaults of her foes.

> "In the Church of Christ, as in every government and properly organized institution on earth, there must exist an ultimate authority, which shall decide when bishops disagree. As a nation has its responsible ruler, a judiciary its supreme court, an army its commander-in-chief, and a ship its captain, so must the Catholic hierarchy have a responsible, recognized head, who shall give a final decision in matters of faith and morals. And this has always been the case. 'I never could understand,' said Robert Suffield, a Unitarian Minister, 'how the Church could be infallible, and its Head liable to be mistaken.'" STODDARD, *Rebuilding a Lost Faith*, New York: P. J. Kenedy and Sons, p. 144).

C. Some Objections Answered

The most unreasonable objections are sometimes heard against the Infallibility of the Pope.

a) Thus it is said: "All men are fallible, therefore the Pope, too, can err." If it were true that all men are fallible, then the Apostles would not have been infallible in their teaching. And yet there cannot be the slightest doubt that the Apostles did claim such an infallibility for themselves. St. Paul was so firmly convinced of his infallibility that he wrote to the Galatians: "If any man preacheth a Gospel other than we have preached to you, let him be anathema" (1:8-9). And St. John writes: "If any one cometh to you and bringeth not this doctrine, receive him not into your house, nor greet him." (*2 John* 10).

Left to themselves, all men may err, but God can certainly protect men from error, whenever and in what manner He pleases, and if He promised to do so, He will keep His promise.

b) We sometimes hear Protestants say: "You Catholics make an omniscient God of the Pope; you might just as well declare him to be almighty."

In reality we regard the Pope only as an instrument of God. If God could inspire the sacred writers of the Bible to write down His revelations infallibly, He can surely also enlighten the Supreme Head of His Church so that he may interpret these same revelations without error.

c) In their efforts to discredit the Catholic doctrine of Papal Infallibility non-Catholics often make the ridiculous assertion that we Catholics believe that the Pope can stamp any statement whatever with the seal of infallibility.

The truth is that the Pope (as well as a General Council) decides all matters of faith and morals according to the tenor of Holy Scripture and Tradition. He only explains the word of God entrusted to the Church in Scripture and Tradition, and condemns the opposite errors.

d) Again Protestants maintain that authority, not conscience, is the Catholic's guide.

This is not true. No infallible Pope or Council can be a substitute for the individual conscience. The Catholic also acts according to the dictates of his conscience. But his conscience is enriched by the directions of the infallible teaching authority. Light and truth are communicated to it. Not only scientific knowledge, but faith, too, is a road to God, and faith rests on infallible authority. Whoever does not recognize the Church as the infallible teacher of divine truth, cannot submit his conscience to her.

e) Non-Catholics love to boast of their freedom, and pity the poor enslaved intellect of the Catholic. Freedom is a very patient and much abused word. It all depends on what we claim to be free from: free from error or free from truth. But the truth alone can make us free. Truth alone can give us the true freedom of the children of God. "If you continue in My word, you shall be My disciples indeed; and you shall know the truth, and the truth shall make you free." (*John* 8:31-32). And in order that this truth, the truth which God revealed to us, "shall not perish from the earth," Christ endowed His Church and her Head, to whom He had entrusted it, with the gift of Infallibility.

The Infallibility of the Popes a Necessity

You will tell me that infallibility is too great a prerogative to be conferred on man. I answer: Has not God, in former times, clothed His Apostles with powers far more exalted? They were endowed with the gifts of working miracles, of prophecy and inspiration; they were the mouthpiece communicating God's revelation, of which the Popes are merely the custodians. If God could make man the organ of His revealed Word, is it impossible for Him to make man its infallible guardian and interpreter? For, surely, greater is the Apostle who gives us the inspired Word than the Pope who preserves it from error.

If, indeed, our Savior had visibly remained among us, no interpreter would be needed, since He would explain His Gospel to us; but as He withdrew His visible presence from us, it was eminently reasonable that He should designate someone to expound for us the meaning of His Word.

A Protestant Bishop, in the course of a sermon against Papal Infallibility, used the following language: "For my part, I have an infallible Bible, and this is the only infallibility that I require." This assertion, though plausible at first sight, cannot for a moment stand the test of sound criticism.

Let us see, sir, whether an infallible Bible is sufficient for you. Either you are infallibly certain that your interpretation of the Bible is correct or you are not. If you are infallibly certain, then you assert for yourself, and of course for every reader of the Scripture, a personal infallibility which you deny to the Pope, and which we claim only for him. You make every man his own Pope. If you are not infallibly certain that you understand the true meaning of the whole Bible—and this is a privilege you do not claim—then, I ask, of what use to you is the objective infallibility of the Bible without an infallible interpreter?

If God, as you assert, has left no infallible interpreter of His Word, do you not virtually accuse Him of acting unreasonably? For would it not be most unreasonable in Him to have revealed His truth to man without leaving Him a means of ascertaining its precise import? Do you not reduce God's Word to a bundle of contradictions, like the leaves of the Sybil, which gave forth answers suited to the wishes of every inquirer?

Of the hundred and more Christian sects now existing in this country, does not each take the Bible as its standard of authority, and does not each member draw from it a meaning different from that of his neighbor? Now, in the mind of God the Scriptures can have but one meaning. Is not this variety of interpretations the bitter fruit of your principle: "An infallible Bible is enough for me," and does it not proclaim the absolute necessity of some authorized and unerring interpreter? You tell me to drink of the water of life; but of what use is this water to my parched lips, since you acknowledge that it may be poisoned in passing through the medium of your interpretation?

How satisfactory, on the contrary, and how reasonable is the Catholic teaching on this subject! According to that system, Christ says to every Christian: Here, My child, is the Word of God, and with it I leave you an infallible interpreter, who will expound for you its hidden meaning and make clear all its difficulties. Here are the waters of life, but I have created a channel that will communicate these waters to you in all their sweetness without sediment of error. Here is the written Constitution of My Church. But I have appointed over it a Supreme Tribunal, in the person of one "to whom I have given the keys of the Kingdom of Heaven," who will preserve that Constitution inviolate, and will not permit it to be torn into shreds by the conflicting opinions of men. And thus My children will be one, as I and the Father are one.

—CARDINAL GIBBONS, *Faith of Our Fathers*,
Baltimore: John Murphy Co., p. 135.

The Human Element in the Church of Christ

The Catholic Church here on earth is not a company of celestial beings, but a society of mortal men, struggling amid the storm and stress of life. . . .

Divine grace and human weakness—here are the materials out of which the Christian life is built up in this world. Many a one makes but an imperfect response to the invitation of Divine grace, and is far removed from the high standard of Christian sanctity. All this is permitted by a merciful God, and is in harmony with His wise designs; thou hast no right to be scandalized by it.

Such are the materials which God chooses for the accomplishment of His work! It is no hard task to build a house with sound stone and good mortar, but to build it of sand is a very different matter.

With a favoring wind and a stout-hearted crew, with well-trimmed sails, and skilful hands at the helm, the ship glides smoothly enough over the waves. But if the seas run high, and a gale is blowing, if the crew turns mutinous, and the rudder snaps, and yet, in spite of it all, the vessel comes safely into port at last, then indeed men hail it as a miracle.

The fact that the Catholic Church has survived the storms of the centuries, that she lives on despite the human infirmities of her rulers and her members, is the clearest proof that her origin is divine.

—TILMANN PESCH, S.J., *Christian Philosophy of Life*, St. Louis: B. Herder Book Co., p. 616.

=====

SUGGESTIONS FOR STUDY AND REVIEW

1. Show that Christianity is not a system of philosophy or human wisdom. What follows from this fact?
2. What is meant by Infallibility? Why did Christ promise Infallibility to His Church?
3. Prove from reason and from history that an infallible teaching authority is necessary in matters of faith.
4. Who constitute the infallible teaching body of the Church?
5. When is the Pope infallible? What is meant by an *ex cathedra* decision? What is meant by the term "to define"?
6. Did the Vatican Council introduce a new doctrine when it defined the infallibility of the Pope?
7. Prove from reason that the Head of the Church must be infallible.
8. On what words of Christ is the infallibility of the Pope based?
9. Answer three common objections against Papal Infallibility.
10. Did Popes Liberius, Vigilius, and Honorius render false decisions in matters of faith? (See the articles in the Catholic Encyclopedia). Was the condemnation of Galileo an infallible decision of the infallible teaching body of the Church? (See *Cath. Encyclop.*, Art. "Galileo.")

11. Compare the *Apostles' Creed* and the *Nicene Creed*. Are
there any Doctrines in the latter which are not contained
in the former? To answer this question, remember that the
body of Catholic Doctrine grows "not like a snowball grows,
but like a tree grows."

CHAPTER VI

Outside the Church
There Is No Salvation

1. The Church is the Body of Christ (*Eph.* 1:22-23), the realization of the kingdom of Christ on earth, the continuation of His work among men. As such she is the *Church of Humanity.* It is her purpose—a purpose essential to her very nature—to incorporate all men of all times and all places with the Body of Christ. In one word, it is the essence of the Church of Christ to be *Catholic.*

But if the Church of Christ is Catholic, world-wide, all-embracing, she must be *exclusive;* that is, she must be *the* Church of humanity, the only Church in which there is salvation for all men.

Because the Church is conscious of being the kingdom of God on earth, of being the Church of humanity, to which all men, according to the will of Christ, must belong if they wish to be saved, she cannot admit that men can be saved also in any other church. If she did so, she would be guilty of disloyalty to herself, of apostasy from her true nature. Either the Catholic Church is *the* Church, *the* Body of Christ, *the* Kingdom of God, or she is nothing at all—a mere sham and make-believe. "One God, one Christ, one Baptism, one Church." Just as there can be no second Christ, so there can be no second Body of Christ, no second manifestation of the Spirit of Christ. The exclusiveness of the Church is rooted in the exclusiveness of Christ, in His claim to be the Bringer of the New Life, the Way, the Truth, and the Life.

2. The early teachers of Christ's doctrines always taught that salvation was to be found only in the one Church of Christ, and they based their teaching on the words of Christ Himself: "If he will not hear the Church, let him be to thee as the heathen and publican," i.e., as no longer a member of Christ's Body, as outlawed from His society. St. Cyprian, the martyr-bishop of Carthage, is the author of the famous phrase which so aptly and succinctly expresses the Church's claim to be the only institution on earth in which salvation is found: *"Extra ecclesiam nulla salus—outside the Church there* *is no salvation."* (*Eph.* 73:21). The opening words of the *Athanasian Creed* are a paraphrase of these words of St. Cyprian: "Whosoever desires to be saved, before all things it is necessary that he hold the Catholic faith; which faith, except every one do keep entire and inviolate, without doubt he shall perish everlastingly." The same truth is expressed in the Lateran Creed and in the profession of faith published by the Council of Florence.

St. Peter's, Rome

3. But are not all non-Catholics and non-Christians condemned to Hell by this doctrine?

The Catholic dogma, "Outside the Church there is no salvation," must be rightly understood. It must not be regarded as an isolated doctrine, but as a part of the whole system of Catholic doctrine; and it must be put in its proper place in this system.

a) It was not originally directed against non-Catholics *as individuals*, but against heretical sects in so far as they are sects. Its purpose is to safeguard the truth that there is only *one* Body of Christ and therefore only *one* Church which possesses and communicates the fullness of the blessings brought to men by Christ. No church set up by men *against* the original Church of Christ can be a means of salvation. In so far as these churches are *non*-Catholic and anti-Catholic, they cannot give supernatural life. None of them can be called a *mater ecclesia*, a "Mother" Church that gives life to her children and nourishes them.

b) But the non-Catholic churches are not *purely* un-Catholic and anti-Catholic. When they separated from the Church of Christ, they took with them and kept a considerable portion of the Catholic treasure of faith and some means of grace, above all the Sacrament of Baptism. The Church has always upheld the validity of Baptism administered by heretics in the name of the Blessed Trinity. She also admits the validity of Holy Orders in the Schismatic churches of the East and in the Jansenist and Old Catholic churches of Europe. In these churches the true Body and true Blood of Christ is received, not because they are the true Church of Christ, but because in spite of their heresy and schism, they have kept a part of the primitive Catholic inheritance. It is the *Catholic* element in these churches that enables them to be a means of grace and salvation.

c) When the Jansenists of the 17th century maintained that the Sacraments administered outside the Church were only *objectively* valid, but not *subjectively* effective; in other words, that "No grace was given outside the Church," their teaching was condemned by Pope Clement XI.

Since the Sacraments administered outside the Church do confer grace, there is no reason why there should not be found outside the Church, for example in the Eastern churches, men and women of marked piety and even holiness of life.

d) According to Catholic teaching the grace of Christ works

not only in those who profess the Christian Religion, but also in *non-Christians,* in Pagans, Jews, and Mohammedans. Every Catholic Catechism speaks of the *Baptism of Desire* as a substitute for *Sacramental Baptism.* Baptism of Desire is an act of perfect contrition combined with an ardent wish, either explicit or implicit, to receive Baptism and to become a member of the true Church. A person who does not know the necessity of Baptism, but *wishes to do all that is required for salvation,* is said to have an *implicit desire of Baptism.* "Every one that loveth is born of God." (*1 John* 4:7).

Since Christ appeared on earth and founded His Kingdom, there is no longer any *purely natural morality.* "Wherever conscience is aroused, wherever man raises his eyes to God and proclaims his readiness to do the Divine Will, the grace of Christ is at work and puts the germ of supernatural life into the soul."

e) Thus we see that God does not refuse grace to anyone in *good faith,* to anyone who is outside the Church through *invincible ignorance;* but it is essential that he must be in good faith. Whoever, *without his fault,* is not a Catholic, but sincerely seeks the truth and keeps the commandments to the best of his knowledge, does not indeed belong to the *visible body* of the Church, but in spirit, as it were, belongs to the *soul* of the Church:* and therefore can be saved. He is not saved *without* the Church of Christ and *against* her, but *through* her. "For the grace of Christ never operates in an isolated manner in this or that person. It always works in and through the unity of His Body." There is no *invisible* Church beside the *visible* one; there is only one true Church of Christ in which both what is visible and what is invisible are organically united.

> "There is only one Church of Christ. She alone is the Body of Christ, and outside of her there is no salvation. She is the ordinary means of salvation** the only source of Light through which the Truth and Grace of Christ stream forth into this visible world of ours. But from this source of Light those also receive who do not know the Church; yea, even those who misconceive her and fight

---

* Since publication of the encyclical *Mystici Corporis* (1943) theologians recognize that it is better to describe such a person as belonging to the Church invisibly, rather than as belonging only to her "soul." —*Editor,* 1990.

** More accurately, she is the only means of salvation, but there is an extraordinary as well as an ordinary way of belonging to her. —*Editor,* 1990.

against her, if only they are and remain in good faith, if only they seek after the Truth honestly and with singleness of purpose. Even if it is not the Catholic Church herself that breaks to them the bread of Truth and Grace, it is none the less Catholic bread that they eat. And whilst eating of it, they become, without knowing it or willing it, incorporated with the supernatural life of the Church. They belong to the soul* of the Church, even though externally separated from her." (CARL ADAM).

4. Although those who are outside the Catholic Church through no fault of theirs can be saved, yet they are deprived of the inestimable advantages enjoyed by Catholics. We must never forget that the Spirit of Christ, the practices which spring out of that spirit, the means appointed by Christ for the regeneration and salvation of mankind, are found in all their original purity, fullness, and power in the Catholic Church, and in her alone. Hence the privilege of being Catholics is a grace for which we can never be sufficiently thankful. How wonderful this privilege is, can be best felt by one who has long groped about in the darkness of unbelief and the half-light of Protestantism, and then found his way suddenly into the "light and kingdom of God."

"When I am asked," writes John L. Stoddard, "what I have found within the Catholic Church superior to all that Protestantism gave me, I find that language is inadequate to express it. One thinks of the familiar metaphor of the stained glass window in a vast cathedral. Seen from without by day, this seems to be an unintelligible mass of dusky glass. Viewed from within, however, it reveals a beautiful design, where sacred story glows resplendently in form and color. So it is with the Church of Rome. One must enter it to understand its sanctity and charm. When I reflect upon that Church's long, unbroken continuity extending back to the very days of the Apostles; when I recall her grand, inspiring traditions, her blessed Sacraments, her immemorial language, her changeless creed, her noble ritual, her stately ceremonies, her priceless works of art, her wondrous unity of doctrine, her ancient prayers, her matchless organization, her Apostolic authority, her splendid roll of Saints and Martyrs reaching up like Jacob's ladder, and uniting earth and Heaven; when I reflect upon the intercession for us of those Saints and Martyrs, enhanced by the petitions of

*See first note on p. 134. —*Editor*, 1990.

the Blessed Mother of our Lord; and, last but not least, when I consider the abiding Presence of the Savior on her altars—I feel that this One, Holy, Apostolic Church has given me *certainty for doubt, order for confusion, sunlight for darkness, and substance for shadow.* It is the Bread of Life and the Wine of the Soul, instead of the unsatisfying husks; the father's welcome, with the ring and the robe, instead of the weary exile in the wilderness of doubt. It is true, the prodigal must retrace the homeward road, and even enter the doorway of the mansion on his knees; but, *within, what a recompense!"* (*Rebuilding a Lost Faith*, pp. 221-222).

Outside the Church There Is No Salvation

"No man can find salvation save in the Catholic Church. Outside the Catholic Church he can find everything save salvation. He can have dignities, he can have the Sacraments, he can sing 'Alleluia,' answer 'Amen,' accept the Gospels, have faith in the Name of the Father, the Son and the Holy Ghost, and preach it too, but never save in the Catholic Church can he find salvation."

—ST. AUGUSTINE, *Sermon to the People of Caesaria*, No. 6.

"We must once more draw attention to and reprobate a very grave error with which some Catholics are unfortunately affected; for some fancy that people who have lived in error, and are strangers to Catholic unity, can attain eternal life. But this is absolutely opposed to Catholic teaching. We, and you, too, know well that those who labor under invincible ignorance of our holy religion, yet keep the precepts of the law of nature graven by God in all men's hearts, who are prepared to obey God, and who lead an honorable and upright life, are able, by the powerful workings of God's light and grace, to attain eternal life. For God, who sees distinctly, who searches into and knows the mind, spirit, habits and thoughts of all men, would never of His supreme goodness and mercy permit anyone to be punished eternally unless he incurred the guilt of voluntary sin. But it is also perfectly well-known Catholic doctrine that no one can be saved outside the Catholic Church, and that those who contumaciously resist her authority and definitions and who obstinately remain separated from the unity of that Church and from Peter's successor the Roman Pontiff, cannot obtain eternal salvation."

—Pius IX, *To the Bishops of Italy*, Aug. 10, 1863.

The Catholic Church the Only True Church

"She is the Holy Church, the One Church, the True Church, the Catholic Church, the Church which strives against all heresies; she can fight; she can never be outfought. All heresies have departed from her—like useless twigs lopped from the vine; but she herself abides in her Root, in her Vine, in her Charity."

—St. Augustine, *De Symbolo*, 14.

"'God is One and Christ is One, His Church is One, His See is One, founded by the voice of the Lord on Peter. No other altar can be set up, no other priesthood instituted apart from that one altar and that one Priesthood. Whoso gathers elsewhere, scatters."

—St. Cyprian, *Ep.* 50, 5.

Suggestions for Study and Review

1. Why must Christ's Church be Catholic?
2. Why must the Catholic Church be exclusive?
3. Who is the author of the expression: "Outside the Church there is no salvation"? On what words of Christ is this doctrine based?
4. Quote the words of the Athanasian Creed which express the same doctrine.
5. Against whom was this dogma primarily directed?
6. Can Baptism be validly conferred outside the Church? What Sacraments besides Baptism are validly administered in the Schismatic churches of the East?
7. Why do we sometimes meet with very pious persons outside the Catholic Church?
8. How can non-Christians be saved?

9. When is a person said to belong to the soul of the Church?
10. Why is it such an inestimable privilege to belong to the Catholic Church?
11. If the Church is tolerant why did she persecute those who fell away from her communion during the Middle Ages?
12. Write a brief paragraph on each of the following: *St. Cyprian, Athanasian Creed, Lateran Creed, Jansenism.*

SUGGESTED READINGS

Stoddard, J. L., *Rebuilding a Lost Faith*, Chs. IX, XIV and XXII.
Russell, W. H., *Your Religion*, Chs. X, XI, and XXI.
Benson, Msgr. R. H., *Confessions of a Convert.*
Kinsman, F. J., *Salve Mater.*
Curtis, G. P., *Beyond the Road to Rome.*
Catholic Encyclopedia, Articles on the *Church* and on *Tolerance.*
Knox, R. A., *The Belief of Catholics*, Ch. XI.
Adam, Karl, *The Spirit of Catholicism.*
Mueller, F. J., *Upon This Rock.*
Conway, *Question Box,* p. 216.
Connell, Francis J., *The Organization and Government of the Church (Four Radio-Hour Addresses).*

Index

✠ SAINT BENEDICT ✠ PRESS

Saint Benedict Press, founded in 2006, is the parent company for a variety of imprints including TAN Books, Catholic Courses, Benedict Bibles, Benedict Books, and Labora Books. The company's name pays homage to the guiding influence of the Rule of Saint Benedict and the Benedictine monks of Belmont Abbey, North Carolina, just a short distance from the company's headquarters in Charlotte, NC.

Saint Benedict Press is now a multi-media company. Its mission is to publish and distribute products reflective of the Catholic intellectual tradition and to present these products in an attractive and accessible manner.

 TAN · BOOKS

TAN Books was founded in 1967, in response to the rapid decline of faith and morals in society and the Church. Since its founding, TAN Books has been committed to the preservation and promotion of the spiritual, theological and liturgical traditions of the Catholic Church. In 2008, TAN Books was acquired by Saint Benedict Press. Since then, TAN has experienced positive growth and diversification while fulfilling its mission to a new generation of readers.

TAN Books publishes over 500 titles on Thomistic theology, traditional devotions, Church doctrine, history, lives of the saints, educational resources, and booklets.

For a free catalog from Saint Benedict Press
or TAN Books, visit us online at
saintbenedictpress.com • tanbooks.com
or call us toll-free at
(800) 437-5876